IRELAND'S OLYMPIANS

BEIJING & BEYOND

'My earliest sporting memory is watching my dad coach a rowing team. I remember asking why one of them wasn't trying . . . the one called the cox. So anytime I thought someone wasn't trying, I called him a cox . . . Mum says I embarrassed my parents a lot as an eight-year-old.'

– Gavin Noble, Ireland's leading triathlete

'We were training in a small town, outside Athens. We had just finished for the day. I had dropped off my coach and physio and I was driving up a small country road. I was hit by a water truck, broke my back in two places.'

– Jamie Costin, international race walker

'I felt my shoulder snap under the pressure of the water. I got swept away, couldn't reach the bank. And I couldn't swim with the dislocated shoulder.'

– Eoin Rheinisch, Olympic canoeist

'That adrenalin you feel before a race, that's not just aggression, or competitive spirit – it's fear as well. Fear of not performing, fear of mistakes, fear of world-class opponents.'

– David Gillick, European Champion

'If a child can't handle doing sport four days a week and doing the Leaving Cert, what are they going to do in real life?'

– Derval O'Rourke, World Champion

IRELAND'S OLYMPIANS

BEIJING & BEYOND

NIALL O'FLYNN

The Collins Press

For Rita O'Flynn

Published in 2008 by The Collins Press
West Link Park
Doughcloyne
Wilton
Cork

British Library Cataloguing in Publication Data

O'Flynn, Niall
Ireland's Olympians : the new generation
1. Coaching (Athletics) - Ireland 2. Athletes - Ireland -
Interviews 3. Sports personnel - Ireland - Interviews
I. Title
796 .0922417

ISBN-13: 9781905172702

Design and typesetting by Anú Design, Tara
Typeset in Bembo 11.5pt
Printed in Malta by Gutenberg Press Limited

Jacket photographs
Front (clockwise from top left): Kenny Egan (*Sportsfile/David Maher*); Derval O'Rourke (*Sportsfile/Brendan Moran*); David Gillick (*Sportsfile/Brendan Moran*); Eileen O'Keeffe (*Sportsfile/Brian Lawless*); Jessica Kuerten (*Sportsfile/Paul Mohan*); *Ghosted images (l–r)*: Sonia O'Sullivan (*sportingheroes.net/George Herringshaw*); Michael Carruth (*Getty Images/Mike Powell*); John Treacy (*sportingheroes.net/George Herringshaw*); Ronnie Delany (*Sportsfile*);
Spine: Derval O'Rourke (*Sportsfile/Brendan Moran*);
Back (clockwise from top left): Jessica Kuerten (*Sportsfile/Paul Mohan*); Róisín McGettigan (*Sportsfile/Brendan Moran*); Derek Burnett (*ISSF*); Peter O'Leary and Stephen Milne (*Fred Elliott*); Eileen O'Keeffe (*Sportsfile/Brendan Moran*); Alistair Cragg (*Sportsfile/Brendan Moran*); Darren Sutherland, centre, (*Sportsfile/David Maher*).

The Taxpayer's Money

'We have to cut out all this amateur crap. It's phoney. We have to be openly professional, money on the table where everybody can see it.'

– Olympic Champion Carl Lewis, 1988

The Melbourne Games in 1956 yielded a glorious Olympic result for Ireland. A rich harvest of five medals – one gold, one silver and three bronze – lifted Ireland to twenty-first position in the nations' table. It was the first time Ireland would win medals at two different sports, athletics and boxing, and the five won by Ron Delany, Fred Tiedt, Tony Byrne, Freddie Gilroy and John Caldwell is still a record total for an Irish team at the Olympic Games.

Incredibly, those five medals came from a team of just eleven athletes, which included Ireland's first-ever woman Olympian, sprinter Maeve Kyle. But, given the economic conditions of the time, the team was lucky to be in Australia at all.

'We each had to pay £200 to go to the Olympics – or our friends had to pay. That was the contribution we made,' recalls Maeve Kyle, who went on to two more Olympics after Melbourne, representing Ireland in Rome and Tokyo. That £200 may not seem much to a modern audience,

Opposite page:
Fencing – one of the Irish Sports Council's fifteen 'focus sports'.

Siobhan Byrne, the first Irish fencer to compete at an Olympic Games since 1992.
(*Sportsfile/Brian Lawless*)

but she puts it in context. 'Our house, two years previously, that we lived in, our home, had cost us £2,000. So it was a tenth of the cost of our home we had to raise to go to the Olympics.'

'It was an era modern people wouldn't understand – how difficult it was to get money,' explains veteran broadcaster Jimmy Magee. 'Freddie Gilroy, the boxer, for instance – the last £115 was collected a few days before he went. They put a penny or tuppence on the pint in Drogheda and District to make up the money for Tony "Socks" Byrne to go.'

Half a century later, and within the lifetime of the 1956 Olympians, the funding of Irish sport has significantly improved. In the four years between the Athens and Beijing Games, the taxpayer has invested over €30 million in high-performance sport – including €9 million in 2008 alone, €2.213 million of which is paid out in direct grants to athletes and teams.

Eleven 'contracted' athletes, those regarded as having medal potential at the highest level, receive annual payments from the Irish Sports Council of between €30,000 and €40,000, with the potential to earn bonus payments on top for world-class performances at major competitions. The country's 'best paid' athletes, who all receive €40,000, include Derval O'Rourke, the 2006 World Indoor Champion in the 60 metre hurdles, Katie Taylor, the Women's World and European Boxing Champion, and Kenneth Egan, the EU Boxing Champion, now ranked in the top 10 in the world. The lightweight four rowing squad, winners of the 2006 Rowing World Cup, each receive €30,000. 'The better you are, the more money you get,' says Kenny Egan. 'It's like a job in the real world.'

The figures pale, of course, beside the €2 million reputedly paid to Ireland's new soccer boss, Giovanni Trapattoni, or the telephone number salaries earned by soccer stars such as Robbie Keane and Damien Duff. And although all but half a dozen Irish athletes are on funding of less than the average industrial wage (€34,000), the grants are recognised as significant by the recipients themselves. 'If you compare the money to other countries it's very good,' says double Olympian Gearoid Towey. The payments, he says, would be similar to those paid to British athletes, but more than paid to most other European rowers. 'The Danish and the Belgians think our grants are awesome,' laughs the Cork man. 'The system is fantastic – the funding and the programme support,' agrees canoe racer Eoin Rheinisch. 'Without the Sports Council, I would not be able to compete on the world stage.'

Below the top earners, twenty 'world class' athletes, those with the ability to reach Olympic or World finals, receive grants of €20,000 each. This group includes track and field athletes such

Irish Institute of Sport chiefs – Seán Kelly and Greg Whyte.
(*Sportsfile/Brian Lawless*)

as Eileen O'Keeffe, Róisín McGettigan, Robert Heffernan, David Gillick, Joanne Cuddihy, Paul Hession and Fionnuala Britton. Boxers Patrick Barnes, Darren Sutherland, Roy Sheahan, Darren O'Neill and John Joe Nevin are also rated 'world class', as is canoeist Eoin Rheinisch and sailors Maurice O'Connell and Ben Cooke. Some of these athletes, particularly those based abroad, also receive additional funding towards their training expenses.

A number of Paralympic athletes, including Jason Smyth, John McCarthy, Michael McKillop, Orla Barry, Garrett Culliton, Lisa Callaghan and Gabriel Shelly also qualify for either 'contracted' or 'world-class' funding.

In addition, more than seventy 'international class' athletes are supported by payments of €12,000 a year. Smaller grants are made to fifty-six development athletes across eleven sports, and ninety-six juniors in thirteen sports are supported as part of a squad.

Athletes in the 'contracted' and 'world-class' categories, those expected to reach finals at Olympics and World Championships, and perhaps to challenge for medals, can expect their funding to continue at the same high level for two years. 'International-class' performers, and those rated developmental or junior, must meet set criteria each year to keep their grants. The grants are paid into an athlete's bank account every three months.

In all, more than 250 athletes, 3 hockey squads and the cerebral palsy football team are supported under the International Carding Scheme, introduced in 1998 and designed to support talent from the junior ranks right through to the elite. The scheme was initially intended to provide financial support to athletes for training, coaching, competition and general expenses. Athletes were given a 'card' with 'credits' to buy various training services. Most of these expenses, however, are now covered by the high-performance units of the various sports, and the grants are intended to cover day-to-day living costs.

Overseeing the carding scheme from 2008 onwards is the new Irish Institute of Sport. Launched in 2006, a quarter of a century after its Australian cousin, the IIS has an ambitious mission statement – 'to produce sporting champions for Ireland'. Born out of the Athens Review, a comprehensive examination of Ireland's high-performance systems in the wake of the medal-less Games in 2004, the institute has taken on the responsibility for creating 'an environment which supports talented Irish athletes and assists them in achieving sustained levels of excellence in elite sport'. The institute also provides athletes with limited medical, sports science and lifestyle support, paying for the first €3,000 each year of an athlete's visits to specialists such as doctors, physiologists, sport psychologists, biomechanists and physiotherapists. There is a contingency fund, too, to pay for more expensive medical procedures.

The system, of course, has its critics, particularly as a number of the athletes rated 'world class' or better failed in various attempts through 2007 to qualify for the Beijing Olympics – while athletes who have successfully achieved Olympic 'A' qualification remain on grants of just €12,000, a third of the industrial wage. There has been particular scrutiny of the case of Paddy Barnes, the first Irish boxer to qualify for the Olympics, who was grant-aided in 2006 but dropped for 2007. The Sports Council's chief executive, John Treacy, has pointed out that the Belfast boxer rose to senior prominence over a very short period of time in late 2007 and that, as a member of boxing's 'High Performance Group', he had been benefiting from the existing support structure. He has also stressed that most 'carded' athletes get much more than their individual grant, because they are also supported by the €6 million pumped into the high-performance programmes of the fifteen 'focus sports' – athletics, boxing, hockey, shooting, rowing, sailing, swimming, cycling, badminton, canoeing, fencing, tennis, golf (ladies and men) and the paralympics.

There has also been criticism that the funding does little to help young athletes with potential, but no results. 'There is nothing there for people trying to break in,' says Gearoid Towey, a former World Rowing Champion. 'You have to make it first before you are funded. So how do you get there? You have to be very resilient to get there without being funded. They should have some sort of system where the person is identified and, if you are meeting whatever set critieria, you should be funded. I do not think you should have to produce a world-class performance to be funded.'

The Irish Sports Council, in response, defends the system. Shane Keane, Programme Executive with the ISC's High Performance Unit, says the aim is 'focused investment'. 'Athletes have to produce results. That's as it should be. The alternative is a system which is subjective, rather than objective. I think there is strong merit in a situation where athletes are clear about what they have to do, and know that before the season starts.' Some 40 per cent of athletes on the carding scheme, he adds, are juniors. 'What we're trying to build is a structure, a pathway for each sport. If we were only concerned with medals, we would just fund the very top.' Swimming, he points out, spends 80 per cent of its funding on its junior and development squads. 'They are building for the future.'

His boss, the ISC's High Performance Manager, Finbarr Kirwan, says this is the 'economics of sport – maximising the return for sports investment'. He accepts that the system needs to be less bureaucratic, but says that where anomalies may occur there is an appeal process. 'We are happy that the amount of money being made available to athletes at particular levels is comparable to other nations. We are not in a position to fund every aspect of an individual's programme, but we believe we are making an impact.' It is right and proper, he says, that athletes must meet certain standards to get funding. 'We do not want to go back to a system where grants are completely subjective, to the days when it was all about who you knew. We have to be objective. We have to have standards and athletes have to hit those standards to be on the programme.'

Athens Olympian Eoin Rheinisch says the system is good, but argues that it needs more flexibility, both in how it deals with young talent, and how it rewards performance. In many sports, he says, as little as a hundredth of a second can separate a medallist from an also-ran, and that result can have a massive effect on an athlete's funding. The Leixlip slalom specialist, who has been as high as No. 8 in the world, is on a grant of €20,000 a year. He says he is not in the sport for the money but recognises, ruefully, that he missed out on the top level of funding this year 'by a whisker'. In 2007, the slalom racer's best result was at the European Championships in Slovakia, where he finished sixth. But it could have been even better. 'I touched a gate on one of my runs, got a penalty – and without that I would have won a bronze medal, and got the full €40,000.' The gap, he says, between the various funding allocations – €12,000, €20,000, €40,000 – is too great. 'Being ninth in the world or fourth in the world gets you the same funding. When it is measured on such a fine line, there should be a case for making a middle ground.'

These are arguments that win some sympathy from the Executive Chairman of the Institute of Sport, Seán Kelly. He has already set up a subcommittee, which counts Eamonn Coghlan among its members, to review the scheme, including the standards set for juniors. 'The financial differential between one band and another may be too much,' he admits. 'We are forcing athletes to get to targets, when we might be better off allowing them to improve gradually.'

Róisín McGettigan, now one of Ireland's best-performing athletes, ranked well inside the top

Ireland's rowing squad (l–r): Gearoid Towey, Eugene Coakley, Richard Archibald and Paul Griffin, after winning bronze at the men's lightweight four A final in the 2006 World Rowing Championships. (*Sportsfile/David Maher*)

fifteen in the world in steeplechase, was one of those who never received any junior grants and who, even as a senior, did not always qualify for funding. 'I know what it's like to worry about money,' says the Wicklow 27-year-old. 'The hardest year was after I graduated from Providence College in 2004 and I did not qualify for any of the grants.' While finishing her Masters, she worked at a variety of part-time jobs – as a college researcher, in a running store, babysitting for a family with five children. She even did some picture framing. 'You don't want to get a full-time job,' she explains, 'because you will not have the flexibility to train and race.' McGettigan, who qualified for the €20,000 'world-class' grant in 2008, says she's 'grateful' for the support, but adds there is a lot of pressure on athletes that if they do not perform to expectations their grants may be cut.

It is a view confirmed by race walker Robert Heffernan, whose funding came under threat after disqualifications in both the Athens Olympics and in the 2005 World Championships in Helsinki. Warnings for lifting both feet off the ground are an occupational hazard for any race walker and disqualifications are routine at the elite level – the Australian 20 km walker, Jane Saville, was disqualified 150 metres from the gold medal in front of her home crowd at the 2000 Summer Olympics. But Heffernan was in a good position in both finals, with realistic expectations of top ten finishes, and was distraught to be dismissed. 'They were the two worst experiences of my life,' says the Cork man. 'All of my funding relied on Helsinki, it was massive. During the race, I was thinking about my funding. My situation financially was so bad.'

On appeal and after some good performances in 2006, Heffernan did not lose his funding and now gets a grant of €20,000 a year, although he estimates his expenses to be in the region of €60,000. The Cork man, who has a young daughter to support, says the cost of living in Ireland is part of the problem and he, too, criticises the fact that athletes have to reach a set standard before they get funding. In the 2007 World Championships, he finished in sixth position, joint highest of all the Irish athletes. He might have pushed up another couple of places, but he was mindful of previous disqualifications. 'My goal was top twelve, just for security. There was a little bit of me that was thinking I will pay something off my Visa, or pay this bill.'

Heffernan's fellow walker, Olive Loughnane, tells a similar story. At the World Championships in Osaka in the 20 km walk, she got a warning card at 11 km, and another at 14 km. One more, and she knew she was out. 'It came at a point when I would have launched an attack. It forced me to hold back. You go from kilometre to kilometre. It stops you attacking.' She also had the very painful memories of being disqualified at the 2005 World Championships, and being unable to finish in Athens. 'It was very important that I finished. I needed to finish in a major championship.'

Loughnane, on course for her third Olympic competition, was twenty-three when she first got on to the carding system, and she has seen a lot of changes over the past decade. 'Things have changed dramatically. Everything is more professional. There are a lot more professional staff, too, in the athletics association.' Her funding is now just €12,000 – '€1,000 a month to live on' – but she recognises that the administrators have a difficult job. 'It is elitist, but where do you draw the line? I can see why they are moving away from direct funding.'

Patsy McGonagle, the Athletics Team Manager, says the funding is 'generous', and that there is 'increasing support' from the Sports Council and the Institute of Sport. He has seen, he says, some significant developments in recent years in Athletics Ireland and praises in particular the 'strong legacy' of the outgoing CEO of Athletics Ireland, Brendan Hackett.

'We are slowly getting our act together. There's been a change in attitude, the introduction of structures and the appointment of dedicated team managers.' The next step, he says, is to build the necessary indoor facilities, adding: 'It's unfortunate, in retrospect, that Bertie did not tear on with his stadium plan. It was a missed opportunity. The country was flying at the time.'

It is a view that is widely held. Former World champion Eamonn Coghlan is on record as saying that it is 'unbelieveable' that Ireland has no proper indoor track and field arena, and that some

Golf – total funding of €448,000 in 2008. (Golfing Union of Ireland & Irish Ladies Golf Union)

Danielle McVeigh, from Kilkeel, County Down, representing Texas A&M University and Ireland at the World University Games 2007. (*Sportsfile/Brian Lawless*)

stadiums here are colder inside than outside. Derval O'Rourke says facilities here pale by comparison with similarly wealthy nations, such as Sweden and Norway.

Announcing the 2008 grants, the Minister for Arts, Sport and Tourism Séamus Brennan said it was important to recognise 'the very major advances of the past few years'. The government, he said, continues to make substantial investment in sport. 'Where once, and not so long ago, Ireland's athletes were at a competitive disadvantage with their international peers, we now provide the funds that allow our athletes compete with the world's best.' The Minister said he would be meeting with the Irish Sports Council, the Olympic Council and the Paralympic Council to make sure 'that every organisation in the country is one hundred per cent behind the team', and added: 'It's important that we recognise that this is taxpayer's money, and that the taxpayer has invested significantly in sport.'

Significant, yes, say Ireland's sporting federations. But sufficient? No. Dave Passmore, the High

Performance Director of Irish Hockey, says the Sports Council 'is giving us everything they can'. But the government, he says, needs to invest more. 'The total budget given to the focus sports is less than some countries would get for hockey,' he says. 'The government needs to see that if sport is a priority we need to invest properly.' He is critical, too, of the 'year-to-year' nature of sports funding. 'In most countries, sports will know the money they're getting for an Olympic cycle, four years.'

'The budget's quite meagre, to be honest with you,' says Swim Ireland's Head Coach, Keith Bewley. 'It just doesn't seem to be available. Not just for swimming – all sports are struggling, really.'

'We live year to year,' confirms walker Jamie Costin, a veteran of the Sydney and Athens Olympic squads. 'You're always making sure, when you come to September or October, that you have your income sorted out for the following year. Things are much better now than what they were before, but there's still a long way to go.'

Derval O'Rourke makes the point that many Irish athletes forsake careers and higher earnings to stay in sport. 'I get paid €40,000. I have a degree and a post-grad. If I got a job, I would be earning more than that. I stress about my mortgage. My office is never closed. So I struggle with people saying I should be unbelieveably grateful for the funding.'

In the run-up to the London Olympics the UK, by comparison, will invest an estimated £600 million (€797 million) in the funding of elite athletes. The British government has committed to spending, between 2006 and 2012, £200 million of public money, £300 million from the lottery and £100 million in sponsorship from the private sector. Some £75 million (€100 million) of that was spent on preparing athletes for Beijing, a support estimated to amount to £45,000 (€60,000) per athlete per year – in addition to their Athlete Personal Awards, or grants, which peak at £25,383, or €34,000.

Seán Kelly, for his part, promises that the new Irish Institute of Sport will provide 'world-class support' to Ireland's elite athletes and players 'so they can perform at European, World and Olympic level'. His early focus has been on supporting the athletes going to the Beijing Olympics. 'Let's see if we can make a difference for them,' says Professor Greg Whyte, the Institute's Director of Sports Science, 'to really give them the opportunity to get into those finals at the Olympic Games.'

In particular, Kelly is keen to tackle the issue of elite coaching – 'the biggest drawback in Irish sport at the moment'. There is, he says, 'a big lack of good coaches all up along the line' – not just for elite athletes, but for promising juniors as well.

He is particularly critical of the 'tendency' for club coaches to start working with a talented athlete as a teenager, then stay with that athlete all the way to Olympic competition. 'That's like a senior infants teacher working with a star pupil right up to university. It makes no sense.' To correct the situation, Kelly says there is a need for specialist coaches 'at different levels' – for children, juniors, developing athletes and elite performers. The institute chiefs plan to bring in world-class coaches from overseas and then, over time, to develop more 'home-grown' coaches. 'The institute is about reaching the highest possible standards, world-class standards,' says Seán Kelly. 'Coaches are nearly more important than athletes. If you do not have top-class coaches, you cannot raise the bar for athletes.'

A budget of €935,000 has been set aside for new institute programmes in 2008, including the establishment of a medical clinic at Cappagh National Orthopaedic Hospital, and an online 'Injury Management System', which will offer injured athletes fast-track treatment.

The institute will have its headquarters at the National Sports Campus in Abbotstown, the first phase of which will be developed over the next four years, and will include:

- A National Field Sports Training Centre with up to twelve pitches and facilities for Gaelic games, soccer, rugby and hockey.
- A National Indoor Training Centre with world-class facilities for some twenty sports.
- Athlete accommodation, sports science and medical facilities.

The Minister for Sport, Séamus Brennan, who signed the key contracts for the 205-acre development in April 2008, said the National Sports Campus Development Authority is also considering a proposal from Athletics Ireland to include in the development a 200-metre indoor athletics track with spectator facilities.

The IIS is also likely to establish a number of regional hubs, perhaps in partnership with third level colleges such as UCD, DCU and the University of Limerick, among others. There may be 'specific universities for specific sports' confirms Seán Kelly, pointing to the UK system where sports are centralised in certain areas – boxing in Sheffield, athletics, netball and cricket in Loughborough. 'If you are preparing teams for international competition you have to have them together,' insists Kelly.

Having studied the systems of other nations, including the UK and Australia, Seán Kelly appreciates that Ireland has much ground to make up, and he refuses to make any false promises: 'People say it takes about ten years for an institute to really make an impact. We hope to do it quicker than that. We have to realise that we are a small country. We have to be realistic. But when you have a high-performance unit, you have to aim for the top and prepare for that – otherwise you've no business being there.'

In certain cases, says the IIS chief, the institute will provide a 'bubble of support' for uniquely talented individuals in minority sports, to send them abroad for coaching and training, instead of funding a whole system. 'It's a sensible way to approach it in Ireland,' he says.

In the coming years, says Kelly, he will also be expecting more from water sports as 'we are an

Darren Sutherland – 'world class'. (*Sportsfile/David Maher*)

island race', and he would like to see a return to our sporting roots. 'We have gone away from most of the traditionally strong sports – the shot, the hammer, the triple jump. You do not need the greatest resources for those, but you do need good coaches.' Track cycling, he believes, may also represent 'great opportunities'.

The current system has the backing of one of Ireland's greatest-ever athletes, Sonia O'Sullivan, who puts it in a historical context: 'There was a big group of very good Irish athletes in the 1980s, and I think a lot of them were self-sufficient and they didn't actually have a lot of support from the federation. Then I was kind of in the in-between section, where you got some support, but it wasn't as structured as it is now, more amateur. I think now the sport has become very professional and people realise what you need. Things that I suppose we went and got for ourselves now are in place for the athletes. I think they should take advantage of all these things that are there for them, because

Top earner – Katie Taylor, Women's World and European Boxing Champion. (*Sportsfile/Ray Lohan*)

when you have such a good backup support you've got all the answers when you have questions.'

One man who stands to gain from the new dawn is David Gillick, twice European Indoor champion at 400 m. 'Every European country has an institute of sport at this stage,' he says. 'To be honest, we're a little bit behind. But I'm all for the institute, I think it's a brilliant idea. And I hope all top-class Irish athletes get involved with it and let them know what we want from it.'

Gillick himself now lives and trains in the UK – a move which he hopes might not be necessary for future generations of athletes. He would like to see a facility where top athletes from a number of different sports could live and train under one roof. 'When you have athletes of a similar calibre aiming for the same things, with similar aspirations, I think you kind of bounce off each other, there'd be a buzz around the place.'

Greg Whyte agrees: 'The one-stop shop mentality is absolutely crucial. An athlete should be able to go to a facility and access all the services that are required for them to excel. A centralised structure round somewhere like Abbotstown is a wonderful opportunity to do that.'

The Olympic Council, for its part, would like to see more athletes training at home. OCI chief Stephen Martin recognises that there will always be individuals and teams who have to spend time overseas, but adds: 'I would prefer to see more of our athletes training and preparing for international competition in Ireland, under the guidance of world-class coaches. The difficulty with people being away is you're not sure exactly what they're up to – who's coaching them, what they're doing, what their programme is. If they need to access coaching overseas this has to be carefully monitored. It's not inconceivable to have an indoor facility in Ireland that can regulate various climatic conditions in a controlled environment. That said, exposure to warm-weather training, and to international competition opportunities, is important.'

Martin, who won gold and bronze medals with the GB Hockey team, says it is crucial, with so few world-class contenders, that the system gives athletes its total support. 'The back-room team is very important. The athletes are doing more full-time training, but it needs to be carefully thought out. More isn't always better, the intensity levels also need to be monitored. A world-class support system should be in place to ensure that we optimise the health and performance of the athletes. Too many athletes don't even get to the start line. It requires a centrally co-ordinated backup system. That's something to look forward to in the future.'

OCI chief Stephen Martin with the gold-medal winning GB Hockey team.

An Irish Dilemma

'It's the Gaelic Athletics Association – there is a tradition of athletics there.'

– Seán Kelly, former GAA President

By far the largest and most popular sporting organisation in Ireland is the GAA. Boasting over 2,500 clubs and some 800,000 members, it dwarfs every other sporting body and reaches into practically every town and parish in the country. Over 180,000 people, meanwhile, play soccer in Irish clubs and schools. Add to that rugby, with 60,000 players in total . . . and you do not have much of a talent pool left for Olympic sports.

'Most of our best athletes are playing our major field sports. I have no doubt about that,' says John Treacy, Olympic silver medallist and chief executive of the Irish Sports Council. 'We are very fortunate that we have people competing in the Olympic Games, but some of our best athletes, there's no question about it, irrespective of the discipline, are on the playing pitches of Ireland.'

That, in turn, has clear implications for Ireland's potential for medal success at Olympic sports. Dr Ben Levine, director of the Institute for Exercise and Environmental Medicine in Dallas, Texas, explains: 'Given a small country, with limited resources, you can't be great at every sport. There's

Opposite page:
Badminton – the national sport in some countries.

Irish badminton internationals Donal O'Halloran (left) and Mark Topping.
(*Ed Smyth*)

just no way, because the absolute number of truly gifted individuals is going to be very small. If all your best athletes are going into hurling and Gaelic football, it reduces the pool of people who are going to be able to play basketball, or the people who are going to be great swimmers, or the people who are going to be great runners, or wrestlers.'

The very success of our native games, Treacy agrees, 'has a tremendous effect' on the potential for other sports to grow and prosper. He adds: 'A lot of sports here in Ireland feel they compete against each other – that's not really very helpful. They are competing for the hearts and minds of the young people when my belief is they're all in this together.'

'When you look at the number of individuals involved in our three major sports, it accounts for seventy per cent, maybe eighty per cent of all our athletes,' says Professor Niall Moyna, the Head of Health and Human Performance at DCU. 'Without a doubt we're losing seventy per cent of potential Olympians to our three major sports, but primarily to Gaelic games. 'It means that our talent pool for Olympic sports is extremely small.'

Professor Moyna, who is himself heavily involved with the GAA, both at DCU and at a national level, says all the major sports compete for youngsters, but they cannot always deliver on the promise of participation for all. 'GAA and soccer, and rugby to a certain extent now as well, they want to get every kid playing their sport. But then when the kid gets to sixteen or eighteen, we don't have the resources . . . if five thousand kids start playing Under 12 in Dublin, do you think we can have five thousand kids playing Under 16? We can't. We don't have the mentors, we don't have the infrastructure. So what happens is a lot of them fall by the wayside. They start in Gaelic games or soccer, but then eventually they get discarded.'

He has a point. Statistics show that most Under 18s involved in sport are playing team games. By the time they are adults, however, they have left those games behind. The 2004 Irish Sports Council/ESRI report, 'Ballpark Figures: Key Research For Irish Sports Policy', found that 22 per cent of Irish adults are completely inactive. Fewer than a third of Irish adults play sport with any regularity – and those who do, play individual and often non-competitive sports. In fact, 76 per cent of sport played by Irish adults is an individual sport, primarily swimming, golf, cycling, keep-fit sessions and recreational walking. In the top five sports, in order of popularity, soccer is the only team game, and a lot of that is five-a-side.

Ireland, of course, is not the only country to have strong domestic games. New Zealand, Pakistan and Malaysia, to name just three, also have a single dominant sport – in rugby, cricket and badminton, respectively. But when you're a small country, whose main games do not transfer to the international stage, there's a double whammy. And that situation is likely to continue because, as Ben Levine, explains, nations do not choose their national sport – people do. 'You've got to ask

Irish hockey captain
Eimear Cregan.
(*Sportsfile*)

yourself, is there some reason why Malaysia should be the home of badminton, or central Americans should be great at baseball, or Norweigans should be great at cross-country skiing? Well of course there is!' Each country has its own socio-economic and cultural pressures, he says, which determine which sports become most important to a population. 'For example, in the United States if you're a great athlete, you don't go into running, what you do is you play basketball, you play football, because your heroes are people like Michael Jordan. Those are the people who you want to be like. And so, in the United States, there's a huge socio-economic pressure to be successful in those big sports. In Kenya, if you want to be a national hero, you become a runner. Those are the people who everybody looks up to, so every athlete wants to be a runner. And all the athletic resources go into running. Why should Pakistan or the Caribbean be expert at cricket? These are socio-economic reasons, rather than physiological or genetic reasons.'

In Australia, where 'Aussie Rules' football is the dominant domestic game, they still manage to achieve high levels of Olympic success – though not, significantly, in track and field. With a few notable exceptions – like Cathy Freeman – Australia has managed to produce precious few track stars, and for many of the same reasons as Ireland. A major problem, say officials, is that really good young athletes – sprinters, jumpers, throwers, the well built, the strong and the quick – are in high demand for professional sports. The promise of an Olympic medal in four years time cannot compare with money on the table, and the dream of football or cricket stardom.

'How many of our very good athletes, our outstanding athletes, are in the AFL [Australian Football League] playing footie?' wonders four-time Olympian Dr Richard (Ric) Charlesworth,

Eileen O'Keeffe –
an example of what
Irish women can do on
the world stage.
(*Sportsfile/Brendan Moran*)

who coached Australia's women's hockey team to the top of the world rankings. 'There are probably some outstanding runners in Australian Rules football that never get the opportunity to be seen at the highest level.'

He tells the story of Nova Peris-Kneebone, one of the 'Hockeyroos' he coached to Olympic gold in 1996. A year after winning the Olympics, she switched sports to athletics, becoming a double gold medalist in the 1998 Commonwealth Games, winning the 200 m sprint and sharing in Australia's

4 x 100 m relay win. She went on to represent Australia at the 1999 World Athletics Championships and the Sydney Olympics. 'She was a good runner,' says Charlesworth, with typical Aussie understatement, 'but we had six athletes in the team who were quicker than her. The point I am making is that I am sure, in every sport, there are athletes there who have the capacity to compete in other sports, but perhaps you never see them.'

Olympic gold medallist Michael Carruth agrees. The smaller sports, he says, need heroes. GAA has the Dublin and Kerry footballers and the Kilkenny hurlers. Soccer has Damien Duff and Robbie Keane. Rugby has Brian O'Driscoll. But, he contends, 'boxing is starting to take off'. He hopes TV coverage of professional fighters like Bernard Dunne, Andy Lee and John Duddy, plus some of the better-known amateurs – boxers like Kenny Egan, Darren Sutherland and Paddy Barnes – will attract youngsters into boxing clubs.

John Treacy, meanwhile, offers a structural solution. He would like to see, he says, 'in an ideal world, a bit of real co-operation'. The GAA, for example, might team up with athletics, to offer children the opportunity to try a wider range of skills for the benefit of both sports. 'Gaelic games can reach out to every parish in the country. Athletics currently can't do that. They don't have the capacity to do it.' It makes sense for GAA clubs to introduce speed and endurance drills, jumping and throwing – they're the sort of skills football and hurling coaches teach anyway. But then, if a child or teenager shows particular promise, they might also point them towards the local athletics club.

'The best sports people in the country have all played different sports, and they are better sports people, and better co-ordinated, when they do concentrate on their main sport,' argues Treacy. 'Athletes that do different disciplines are better athletes when they concentrate on their main sport, because they learn the basics for all the different sports. And then when they choose to select a sport, they're better then able to cope.'

His suggestion has the support of All-Ireland winner Enda McNulty, who played a major role when Armagh won the football title in 2002. 'Sports bodies should work together,' he says. 'Why not create a massive partnership between athletics and the GAA? Everybody wins. If you want to develop elite world-class athletes it must begin at three to ten years of age.'

Seán Kelly, the former President of the GAA, now Executive Chairman of the Irish Institute of Sport, points out that athletics has always been a traditional Irish sport, dating back to the Tailteann Games.

In fact, newspaper reports of a foundation meeting for the GAA in November 1884 record that hurling and football were never mentioned. The *Cork Examiner* reported at the time that the meeting was dominated by talk of athletics and discussed proposals for an athletics competition for Celtic peoples. Founder member Michael Cusack told the meeting that he had tried to get

Catriona Carey moved from camogie to hockey, and won seventy-two caps for Ireland. (*Sportsfile*)

'Girls are more focused, and better at multi-tasking,' says Derval O'Rourke, who says young women need to be more aware of the opportunities available to them in sport, especially the number of grants and scholarships. The smaller numbers playing women's sport give 'competitive animals' a good chance of making their mark, she says. She would also like to see greater 'integration' between the GAA and other sports.

Talent identification expert Chelsea Warr confirms that for women 'there might appear to be more opportunities where greater impact may be made'. She adds: 'Because girls reach physical maturity earlier than boys it's easier to predict their potential.' Physiologist Niall Moyna agrees: 'I believe it's a more level playing field for women. There is no dominant racial group dominating in medals. The performances are within range.'

Dave Passmore, the High Performance Director of Irish Hockey, claims that for Irish women, his sport is the biggest international team game. Ireland's women are ranked fourteenth in the world. But with more funding and better talent identification, they might well go higher. 'There are hundreds of women out there who could make a difference for us. A lot of girls play hockey to twelve or thirteen, then stop. We need to be appealing to them, looking for girls and women who are athletes, with pace and agility.' Hurlers and camogie players, he agrees with Greg Whyte, are easily turned into hockey players – they have the necessary hand–eye co-ordination, and they're used to a fast game. Irish hockey, of course, has already made some significant 'steals' from the GAA. Irish captain Eimear Cregan, for example, from Limerick, is a niece of legendary player and coach Eamonn Cregan.

Cycling experts, meanwhile, are targeting specific events for women riders. 'No nation has a real history in women's track cycling,' says Frank Campbell, the Olympic Team Manager. 'We are looking very hard at putting a women's pursuit team together.'

On the financial front, officials and athletes from several sports have expressed concerns that the new grants for GAA players will hit the funding of Olympic sports. 'The GAA is a multi-million euro organisation,' says double Olympian Gearoid Towey, who says the new National Rowing Centre, impressive though it is, pales by comparison with the facilities of many GAA clubs. 'I have no problem with the GPA [Gaelic Players' Association] getting money, but it should stay within their own organisation.'

'It's ridiculous,' adds one senior official, who is reluctant to be named. 'GAA is not an international performance sport. If the government wants to give them money, good luck to them, but take it out of somewhere else.'

He adds: 'Our funding is the same as last year, and this is an Olympic year, when you'd expect it to increase. You'd also expect a bigger increase for the development of young athletes, with London in mind. This has impacted on Olympic sports. There is no getting away from it.'

The player grants, which will make €3.5 million available to inter-county players, come after five years of campaigning by the Gaelic Players' Association. There is also some opposition to the grants from within the GAA community, but the GPA has welcomed the grants as 'a landmark decision', which merely puts GAA players and the GAA 'on a par with other sports'. GPA chief executive Dessie Farrell has consistently argued that it is discrimination not to give top footballers and hurlers some form of grant-aid, when professional sports people get tax breaks and athletes from Olympic sports receive grants. Players are likely to receive between €1,400 and €2,500, depending on their championship progress. The Minister for Arts, Sport and Tourism, Séamus Brennan, has insisted that the GAA grants are completely separate and will be provided for by extra funding.

That, however, has not stopped the criticism. Several senior athletes, although reluctant to comment on the record, suggest that the GPA grants are already impacting on funding. 'The government gave the Sports Council an extra €3.3 million in 2008. The GPA are getting €3.5 million. You do the maths,' says one veteran Olympian, who complains that he has been left thousands of euro short in promised money to pay his coach. 'It's embarrassing. You are involved in a business relationship and you have to tell someone they are not getting the money they were promised.'

'My support has been cut in half. It was the GAA that screwed it up,' adds another senior athlete.

'The same money has to stretch. Too many of us did well in 2008,' says a third. 'There is nothing for the developing athletes behind us.'

The Irish Sports Council, for its part, denied that any Olympic athlete would be left wanting in the run-up to Beijing. 'No athlete who has qualified has suffered financially this year in any way,' says Finbarr Kirwan, the ISC's High Performance Manager.

While Ireland debates the issues, however, others pounce. Australian football clubs such as Collingwood, Carlton, Sydney and Brisbane already have an extensive scouting network in Ireland, recruiting the likes of Martin Clarke, Kevin Dyas (Collingwood), the Ó hAilpín brothers, Michael Shields (Carlton), Brendan Murphy, Tadhg Kennelly (Sydney), Colm Begley and Pearce Hanley (Brisbane). There are reports, too, that an Australian sports agency is planning to employ an All-Ireland network of scouts, who would offer Irish talent to Aussie Rules clubs.

According to the *Herald Sun*, Australia's biggest daily newspaper, the project is the brainchild of former Aussie Rules player Ricky Nixon, who is now one of the code's leading agents. He's written to all sixteen AFL clubs, telling them of his plans to base a recruiter in each of Ireland's thirty-two counties to identify the best young players aged between fourteen and twenty. He is proposing to charge clubs a little under €20,000 a year for access to the talent database.

'Yes, we're nicking them back to Australia, aren't we?' laughs Dr Ric Charlesworth, High

Performance Consultant with the Freemantle Dockers AFL club. He says it is inevitable that some of the GAA's most outstanding athletes will move into professional sport. It is also possible, he adds, that some Gaelic players will look for opportunities outside their domestic games – in sports that offer them the chance to represent their country, to be involved in international competition or the Olympics. 'In this country, you've got Gaelic games, Gaelic football and hurling, which just about covers everything – running, jumping, kicking, hitting, catching, throwing, all of those things. That's a pretty good background for almost any sport.' He warns, however, that GAA is, clearly, the public's first choice for sport, and that should never be forgotten. 'I think you have to look at where your best chances are and you have to prioritise where you are going to put your resources. But the other side of that is let's also support the games that are popular already and have support, that people are involved in and the people love to play. You have got to do that too.'

Playing to Strengths

For three weeks every four years, the eyes of the world turn to the Olympics. Seven million spectators will attend the Beijing Games, with as many as four billion watching on TV.

For many armchair experts, however, the games will not really catch fire until the second week, when the blue-riband athletics events take to the track and field.

The truth is, however, that of the 302 gold medals to be awarded in the Olympics, just 47 can be won in athletics. A mere 34 are up for grabs in swimming, another of the highest-profile sports. Combine the two, and add up all the gold, silver and bronze medals available, and you come up with 243. That's 243 medals, from a total of some 930.

The point is that there are many, many medals to be won in the Olympics – a majority of them *outside* of the glamour events. And a medal is a medal. A successful nation takes its place on the medals table, regardless of the sport in which that medal is won.

Recognising this, many nations have had significant success targeting events outside the mainstream, or by playing to their national strengths. Denmark has done well in badminton, handball and shooting, Sweden at jumps, Holland in hockey and cycling. In Athens, Australia finished fourth in the medals race, without winning a single athletics gold. Its strongest sports were swimming, cycling, diving and rowing.

Opposite page:
Irish boxers Kenneth Egan (left), John Joe Joyce (centre) and Darren Sutherland in Athens, Greece, after winning three gold medals at the Olympic Qualifying tournament in April 2008. (*Sportsfile/David Maher*)

Internationally, many experts suggest that an ambitious smaller nation might look to concentrate on sports that might be 'soft' internationally, less developed, or with fewer nations competing. 'Small nations like New Zealand and Sweden, if they want to perform well on the world stage they will always play to their strengths,' says Chelsea Warr, a physiologist who has worked with the Australian Institute of Sport and with UK Sport.

It is a point that is not lost on those at the coalface of sport. Derval O'Rourke, for example, would like to see the Irish system recruiting top coaches and targeting the more technical events. 'If you look at other small countries, like Sweden, it's the technical events they are specialising in.'

'If you're a small country, like we are in South Africa, you have to divvy up your resources according to the genetic ability of the population,' confirms Professor Tim Noakes, a co-founder of the Sports Science Institute of South Africa. 'It makes no sense, in my view, for Irish people wanting to win the gold medal in the one hundred metres – it just doesn't make sense. You'd be much better off doing things that you'd been successful with in the past.'

Professor Niall Moyna, DCU's Senior Lecturer in Exercise Physiology, agrees: 'We have to be realistic. How many Olympic medals have we won in track and field? Six. So let's get expectations in perspective, before we start talking about winning a lump of medals. That's not where we are.'

Taking past performance in major championships as a guide, the statistics suggest that Ireland's best Olympic hopes might lie in shooting, rowing, middle-distance running, boxing, hammer throwing and cycling.

In 2007, Ireland's best sporting performance in world terms came in a minority sport: clay pigeon shooting. At the World Shotgun Championships in Cyprus, Ireland won individual silver and team bronze, the best result in Irish shooting history. Philip Murphy from Carlow took the individual silver medal, hitting a personal best score of 145 out of 150 targets to secure second place behind double Olympic and World champion Michael Diamond of Australia. Murphy also added a team bronze with Olympians David Malone and Derek Burnett. Not bad for a team aged forty-nine, forty-three and thirty-six, respectively! Derek Burnett also won an individual silver medal during 2007, at the ISSF World Cup in Maribor, Slovenia.

Other sports in which Ireland is traditionally 'world class' include boxing, rowing and cycling. Of the twenty medals Ireland has won in the Olympic Games, no fewer than nine have been taken home by Irish boxers. A further five Irish fighters have won medals at the World Championships. That is a proud tradition, and one which is being built on to this day. In fact, if women's boxing were an Olympic sport, Ireland would go to Beijing as one of the favourites for the lightweight gold medal, in the person of Katie Taylor, the reigning World and European champion.

Taylor, from Bray in County Wicklow, won the 60 kg World Championship in 2006 and the last three European titles – 2005, 2006 and 2007. She is also an international soccer player. 'It's very disappointing, very frustrating, really, looking at the lads training for the Olympics, and I know that I can't be there with them,' she told RTÉ's Marty Morrissey at the World Boxing Championships in Chicago. 'But I'm nearly sure now that it's going to be in, in 2012, so that's something for me to train for, to look forward to. So I'm going to stay amateur until the London Olympics and hopefully win the gold medal there.'

Katie, currently ranked the best pound-for-pound woman boxer in the world, has every chance of fulfilling her dream says Performance Director Gary Keegan: 'If women's boxing was an Olympic

sport, she would be an undisputed medal prospect. Going in with her record over the last four years, she would be the girl to beat. She is totally dominant in her weight category.'

Throwing his weight behind the push to have women's boxing included in the 2012 Games is a very influential figure, the President of the European Olympic Committee, Ireland's own Pat Hickey.

Hickey says he is confident that the female version of the sport will be given the go-ahead for the London Olympics. 'I will be doing everything in my power to try and ensure that women's boxing is an Olympic sport in 2012,' says Hickey, who is also the President of the Olympic Council of Ireland. 'Katie is a superb athlete and she deserves the chance to represent Ireland on the highest stage of them all and I will be lobbying the powers that be from here on in to ensure that women's boxing is included in London.'

Katie Taylor, of course, is not the only success story in Irish boxing. Since January 2006, Irish boxers have claimed over eighty-five gold, silver and bronze medals at international tournaments. At the 2007 European Union Championships in Dublin, Irish boxers won three gold and two silver medals. In one magnificent day at the National Stadium, in front of a delighted home crowd, light heavyweight Kenneth Egan, middleweight Darren Sutherland and welterweight Roy Sheahan all became EU champions. Carl Frampton and Cathal McMonagle added the silvers. Irish underage boxers also took medals at the 2007 European Schoolboys Championships and the European Cadet Championships.

In Beijing, Ireland will be represented by five boxers, a vast improvement on Athens 2004, where Limerick middleweight Andy Lee was our sole representative, and on Sydney 2000, where Cork man Michael Roche was Ireland's only boxer.

It is a strong team, too, with three of the Irish ranked well inside the world's top 15 boxers, in their respective weight categories. Four of the five have won Olympic qualifying tournaments in the run-up to Beijing.

Ireland's Beijing contenders are:

- Light Heavyweight: Irish captain Kenneth Egan (twenty-six), Dublin – World No. 9, EU champion, European bronze medallist (2006), winner of eight senior Irish titles, gold medal list at the Olympic qualifying tournament in Athens, Greece.
- Middleweight: Darren Sutherland (twenty-six), Dublin – World No. 12, EU champion, winner of five Multi Nations gold medals, gold medallist at the Olympic qualifying tournament in Athens, Greece.
- Light flyweight: Paddy Barnes (twenty-one), Belfast – World No. 14, the first Irish fighter to qualify for the Games, by reaching the quarter-finals of the World Boxing Championships.
- Bantamweight: John Joe Nevin (eighteen), Cavan – in his first senior competition in an Irish vest, won a gold medal at the Olympic qualifying tournament in Pescara, Italy.
- Light welterweight: John Joe Joyce (twenty-one), Athy, a European Junior bronze medallist and two-time Leinster handball champion, gold medallist at the Olympic qualifying tournament in Athens, Greece.

The Irish captain, Kenny Egan, says that, for a nation of 4 million people, Ireland has done well to qualify so many boxers. He is quietly confident, too, about the team's chances – predicting that Beijing could see Ireland's best boxing performance since the Barcelona Games in 1992, when Michael Carruth won the welterweight gold medal and Wayne McCullough the bantamweight

From left to right:
(l–r) Irish boxers John Joe Joyce, Kenneth Egan and Darren Sutherland; Kenneth Egan, left, celebrates with Darren Sutherland after winning their semi-finals at the final Olympic Qualifying tournament in Athens, Greece. (*Sportsfile/David Maher*)

silver. 'Now that we have five, people are starting to think "well hang on now, we have five boxers going to the Olympics. Are there going to be medals here?" The standard that we have in the team now, the five that qualified are well capable of going there and pulling medals.'

Two hundred and eighty-six boxers will compete in Beijing, but no more than thirty-two in any weight category. For Egan and his team-mates, that's five fights to win, in an unseeded, open draw, which includes quite a number of fighters they have previously beaten. 'I hope just to come out and perform. I am not going to say I want to get to a podium or win medals. But if I'm relaxed, anything can happen.'

It will not be easy, though, in a sport now dominated by the Russians and Cubans, and by boxers from former USSR republics such as Uzbekistan and Kazakhstan. At the Athens Games, there were high hopes for Limerick middleweight Andy Lee, a European bronze medallist. He lost, however, in the second round. The Irish Sports Council's 'Athens Review' had this to say about the changing circumstances in the sport: 'Boxing is considered to be a strong event for Ireland, as a result of its previous medal success at the Olympic Games of 1952, 1956, 1964, 1980 and 1992. However, following the break-up of the Soviet Union, the process of qualifying boxers out of Europe for the Olympic Games has become considerably more arduous – meaning that the circumstances in which that historical success was achieved were wholly different to the present.'

The current resurgence in Irish boxing, says Egan, has much to do with the Irish Amateur Boxing Association's new High Performance system. Launched in 2002 and overseen by Performance Director Gary Keegan, the High Performance Group now runs four separate programmes:

- Senior – sixteen boxers, split into elite and pre-elite groups
- Women – Katie Taylor
- Cadet – twenty-one boxers, aged fifteen to seventeen
- Junior – twenty-one boxers, aged seventeen to nineteen

In 2008, the IABA received €550,000 in Irish Sports Council funding for its high-performance programe, plus a contribution of €70,000 to a junior fund. A further €315,000 is paid out to some forty boxers supported by the Carding Scheme, which awards individual grants ranging from €3,000 for promising juniors up to €40,000 for Katie Taylor and Kenneth Egan. The boxers also have access to sports science, medical, nutritional and other supports.

Most of the top boxers live and train at the National Stadium, under the eye of Ireland's head coach, Billy Walsh, and his No. 2 from Georgia, Zaur Antia. A third coach, Jim Moore, looks after the juniors and cadets.

From left to right: Ireland's John Joe Nevin raises the Tricolour after winning the gold medal at the AIBA European Olympic Qualifying Tournament in Pescara, Italy, in March 2008 (*Sportsfile*); Ireland's bronze-medal-winning team at the 2007 World Shotgun Championships: from left, in green, David Malone, Philip Murphy, Derek Burnett. (*ISSF*)

For Kenny Egan, the new system is a sea change from what was there in previous times. 'It's more professional, without a doubt,' he says. 'When I won my first senior title in 2001 there was no structure, no high-performance programme set-up. You won your senior title, you probably went to a training camp and then went to World or European championships. Now it's a lot more professional. We have our doctors, physiotherapists, sport psychologists - and it's all on call. That's been a big help.'

A key development is that any injuries are now looked after right away. When Olympic contender Roy Sheahan broke his hand at a training camp in Italy one Sunday in February, he was on the operating table in Dublin at 8 a.m. on Tuesday morning. 'In the old days,' says Egan, 'you might not even have a doctor.'

The high-performance programme is highly sophisticated, and there is a daunting competition schedule. Irish boxers were scheduled to fight at twenty-three events in 2008, including nine major championships. Four international training camps were planned: Italy, for the Seniors, Kazakhstan (Youths), Germany (Cadets) and Norway, for Katie Taylor. Ireland's system is also attracting international interest, and the French and British federations have both sent teams to train with the Irish in Dublin.

In the past, says Kenny Egan, Irish boxers probably fought around half a dozen internationals a year. 'Now, with the high-performance programme, we are probably clocking up fifteen to twenty. That's a big difference . . . the organisation that goes into it, the travelling, the training camps, the sparring camps, there's a big difference. We have links now with Poland, France, Germany and especially Russia – probably the best amateur team in the world.'

The Irish men's heavyweight four: Alan Martin (centre), Sean O'Neill (left), Cormac Folan (right) and Sean Casey (hidden). (*Sportsfile/David Maher*)

Egan's team-mate, Darren Sutherland, is equally unbeat about the new Irish system. 'We train like professionals – twice a day, six days a week. The whole set-up is constantly improving. The future is bright for the younger lads coming through it. It's a very, very professional set-up, probably one of the best. Very few sports in Ireland have the same professional set-up that we have. Every area is catered for. It's a great team. I am happy to be a part of it.'

The Irish coaches, meanwhile, can draw on some of the most up-to-date training aids. Performance Analyst, Alan Swanton, for example, provides a comprehensive attack analysis of all the Irish fighters, plus the world's best four fighters at every weight division, showing the punches they throw, the combinations, and how often they attack. 'The best boxers in the world launch an attack, on average, under every four seconds, or even faster,' says Gary Keegan. When the high-performance programme started, Irish boxers were only attacking every six and a half to seven seconds. This has dramatically improved, with Keegan insisting that, whatever else they lack, the Irish boxers will be in peak physical condition and mentally strong. 'We can become world class in our physical preparation of the team,' he says. 'If you are physically strong, mentally strong and technically short, you can still do the business.'

Keegan, however, would like to see the high-performance programme become even more focused. At the moment, he says, the programme is playing two roles, catering for two tiers of boxers: the elite senior squad and the most promising youngsters. In many cases, he says, the elite set-up does not best serve some of the younger boxers. 'The programme may be too advanced for them, but there is nowhere else for them to go.' The next step, says Keegan, is to give the developing boxers their own separate programme, underpinning the high-performance programme, which would provide a better 'pathway' to the international set-up.

He has proposed that the IABA set up a system of regional 'centres of excellence', to underpin the high-performance system. For an estimated cost of €250,000 per year, he says, the association could provide such centres in each of the provinces, plus Dublin and Belfast, where boxing is particularly strong. The centres would be based in existing clubs and be staffed by a regional head and five coaches who would work part-time, twenty hours a week. This, he says, would provide a better service to the best youngsters from Ireland's 265 boxing clubs who, to take part in the evolving Cadet and Junior programmes, must currently travel up to Dublin from all over the country. 'This structure would allow us to provide the correct level of coaching to this talented group and also allow us to educate coaches at source.'

It is an idea which has won the support of Olympic gold medallist Michael Carruth. Strong boxing clubs such as Drimnagh in Dublin, Holy Trinity in Belfast, Athy in Kildare and Clonmel in Tipperary would be ideal homes for such 'centres of excellence', he says, pointing to the success that another sport – rugby – has had in the provinces. 'This would bring both boxers and coaches to a new level.'

'We need to be thinking more long term,' says Gary Keegan. 'There is no short-term solution to high performance. We have to improve the standards of coaching, improve the standard these kids are at when they enter the programme. The basic building blocks are missing.' Club coaches, he says, focus too much on teaching punches, and not enough on footwork or co-ordination. 'Coaches can be overly focused on competition and winning and this can impact negatively on the young boxer receiving the time and opportunity to develop the fundamentals which greatly support his ability to fulfil potential in the long term.'

Keegan would like to see a greater concentration on teaching skills to pre-teens. From the age of thirteen onwards, however, he says Irish boxers should go into multi-age competition – thirteen- and fourteen-year-olds together, and fifteen- with sixteen-year-olds. That, he says, would better stimulate the most promising boxers and prepare them for international junior competitions.

Rowing, too, is one of Ireland's most successful sports. Since 1991, Irish crews have won a total of fifteen World Championship medals – four gold, five silver and six bronze. There has also been significant success at Under-23 and Junior level.

The pride of the fleet, in recent years, has been the men's lightweight four, which has made the final of two of the last three Olympics – finishing fourth in Atlanta and sixth in Athens. In 2006, the current four – Gearoid Towey, Paul Griffin, Richard Archibald and Eugene Coakley – won the overall Rowing World Cup and took a bronze medal at the World Championships.

Fuelled by that success, the Irish Amateur Rowing Union (IARU) opened a new National Rowing Centre at Inniscarra in Cork in May of 2007, to serve as a centre of excellence for Irish rowing's high-performance programmes. The €5 million centre boasts five large boat bays to house the national team equipment, an elite strength and conditioning room, a training gym, plus sports science, physiology, recovery and medical facilities. 'As recently as four years ago we had a lake, but no facilities at all,' says Mike Heskin, Irish Rowing's International Team Manager. 'Our athletes were togging out in the back of cars.' Now, he says, they are planning the next phase: a residential unit, so that the top rowers can live on site.

The European Junior Championships, the 'Coupe de la Jeunesse', will be staged at Inniscarra in 2008. A number of top international teams have also expressed interest in using the National Rowing Centre's facilities. Irish heavyweight coach Harald Jahrling is not surprised: 'This is a top-class training facility comparable to those of the world's top rowing nations. It's no wonder that a number of those nations want to come here for training camps.'

It was against that background that the 2007 World Rowing Championships in Munich were a huge disappointment for Ireland, which sent thirteen rowers in six boats – but secured only one Olympic place, the men's heavyweight four of Alan Martin, Sean Casey, Sean O'Neill and Cormac Folan.

The standard, say the rowers, is extremely high. 'All the top guys from around the world are coming back to try to qualify for Beijing,' Alan Martin told RTÉ in Munich. 'Each country has stacked their boats. The standard is so much higher. In the 'C' final there were Olympic medallists. Every event is the same. There's going to be no easy qualification.'

'Staying at the top in rowing has become harder and harder,' agrees team manager Mike Heskin. He admits, though, that the Irish squad had 'problems' in the run-up to the World Championships, and that both the athletes and the coaching staff were stretched too much. In the wake of Munich, where the lightweight four finished last in the 'B' final, rowing bosses made swingeing changes –

Swimming – there are thirty-four gold medals to be won in the pool at the Olympics.

Tralee's Florry O'Connell at the World University Games 2007, Bangkok, Thailand. (*Sportsfile/Brian Lawless*)

wooing back double Olympian Gearoid Towey, appointing Heskin, and bringing in a dedicated lightweight coach, John Holland, who worked with the lightweight four in Atlanta, and coached the Greek lightweight double to a bronze medal in Athens.

'I was in Spain, in Barcelona, watching the World Championships,' recalls Towey, who had been out of competitive rowing since January 2006. 'Looking at the 'A' final, I saw crews in that final we had beaten in 2006. There were some crews in that final that never came near us. I said to myself, this is do-able. It reinforced my decision to come back. I went down to the rowing club in Barcleona and trained the next day.'

'We have the crew back who rowed in 2006,' says Heskin. 'There is a balance. The competitiveness of the other three is fantastic – there's Paul Griffin's drive, Archibald's total focus on

Born in Ireland, Made Overseas

In the spring of 2006, two men sat listening to a Powerpoint presentation . . .

It was a powerful production, and Finbarr Kirwan and Brendan Hackett could not but be impressed.

As the High Performance Manager of the Irish Sports Council, and the CEO of the Athletics Association of Ireland, the two men were well used to athletes looking for extra funding. But this was different: professional, a business proposal – money in, medals out.

The two men listened as David Gillick argued his case. As a very promising athlete, already the European Indoor Champion, he told them he simply could not make the step up to elite world level by training at home in Ireland. He had investigated the possibilities, and had been asked to join a world-class training group at Loughborough University, in Leicestershire in England, under the top UK sprint coach, Nick Dakin.

'I had already made the decision to move,' he recalls. 'I had to get into an environment where I was training full-time. I didn't want to get to the age of thirty and ask myself why I didn't give myself a real chance in athletics. I didn't want to be looking back and wondering what might have been if I put my neck on the line.'

Opposite page:
Ireland's leading triathlete,
Gavin Noble.
(*Gordon Thompson*)

For an investment of €15,000, for coaching fees, facilities, rent and bills, Gillick told the two managers that he could guarantee them world-class performances over the period leading to the Beijing Olympics. They gave him the lot.

'In many ways, David was ahead of his time,' says Finbarr Kirwan. 'It was interesting to see him take this step. He realised he wasn't simply entitled to the money. But he made a compelling case that there would be a return from this investment. It was a very mature way to reflect the situation.'

Shortly afterwards, David Gillick moved out of home and went to live and train as a full-time athlete at Loughborough. 'One day I decided I was going to the UK. Two weeks later, I was over there. It all happened really quickly,' he recalls.

He joins a growing band of Irish athletes who have settled overseas in recent times, convinced that, if they are to make an impact on the world stage, they need to live and train at the highest level. And that, more often that not, means leaving Ireland.

In fact, of the fifteen athletes who made up the Irish team for the World Athletics Championships in Osaka in 2007, all but three are now regularly training abroad, most of them in the UK or the USA, but others in Europe, South Africa and Australia.

Alistair Cragg, Róisín McGettigan and Mary Cullen are all based in the USA: Cragg is in Arkansas, McGettigan and Cullen move between New England and Florida. Cavan 800 m runner David Campbell is in Melbourne, training with Sonia O'Sullivan and Nic Bideau. Derval O'Rourke is in Bath. Paul Hession is training with Stuart Hogg's squad in Scotland. Walkers Rob Heffernan and Jamie Costin have been winter training in Spain and altitude training in South Africa. Their Leitrim counterpart, Colin Griffin, is based in Italy. And training with David Gillick in Loughborough are hurdler Michelle Carey and Kilkenny sprinter Joanne Cuddihy.

Though the situation speaks volumes about the lack of elite training facilities in Ireland, and the scarcity of world-class coaches, there are many, both athletes and officials, who say that a 'brawn drain' has always been a part of Irish sport and may continue to be so into the future – and that this is not necessarily a bad thing.

'If we find that there's an athlete who we think can train and compete at a higher level outside of Ireland, then we're going to support them,' says Kirwan.

His boss, the ISC chief executive, John Treacy, agrees: 'If you're a technical person, and you're down in Belfield in the wintertime, and it's wind and rain, sure what technique could you do? So there is a need for our athletes to go overseas and train and the Sports Council provides that opportunity. It will always be so, absolutely, particularly if you're involved in an outdoor sport. People will always be coming and going.'

Ireland, of course, is not alone in exporting its athletes. An estimated 200 Australian athletes,

for example, are currently involved in elite sport in Europe. The Australian Institute of Sport has developed a European training centre close to Milan, where athletes can base themselves, and travel to train and compete. 'In some disciplines, in the cycling and winter sports, you don't have the conditions or the environment that is appropriate in Australia, so it makes sense,' says top Australian coach Ric Charlesworth, who points out that Australia's geographical isolation makes it difficult for athletes and teams to get regular international competition. 'In terms of finding the right place for each athlete in each discipline, you need a great deal of variety.' Sweden, meanwhile, has done very well in golf, despite the fact that the sport cannot be played in Sweden in the wintertime. 'That's not a reflection on Sweden,' says John Treacy. 'It's just a fact of life.'

Treacy, twice World Cross Country champion and an Olympic silver medallist, says he learned during his time in America that it was often easier to focus on training when he removed himself from his home place. 'I'm a big believer in this – if being in a training environment lends itself to hard work, sometimes you need to get away from your own base, your own home, your own place where you're comfortable, to focus on training. I used to do that as well.'

'It's a positive thing,' insists Patsy McGonagle, the Athletics Team Manager for the Olympics. 'These athletes have looked at the situation and, over a period of eighteen months, several members of the team have moved to different environments. In some cases they've moved to get out of their comfort zone, or moved to an appropriate training group. Some of them have moved for technical reasons, some of them have needed a fresh approach. Some of them have made the move for climatic reasons.'

From left to right: Dubliner Barry Murphy, swims out of the University of Tennessee (*Sportsfile/Brian Lawless*); Walker Rob Heffernan celebrates his sixth-place finish at the 2007 World Championships. (*Sportsfile/Brendan Moran*)

The current trend, he says, started after the 2006 European Athletics Championships in Gothenburg, Sweden, a meet that was saved from mediocrity by Derval O'Rourke's silver medal in the 100 m hurdles.

Ireland's athletes, says McGonagle, started to realise that they needed certain advantages if they were to compete at the highest level. They looked jealously across at the UK, where their British counterparts have access to a choice of world-class facilities in centres such as Loughborough, Bath, Stirling and Cardiff, with accommodation on campus, and the backup of coaching, medical and science support. 'Ireland doesn't have a high-performance centre, we don't have indoor facilities. There is a serious need for those.' He contends that the current group could not be doing more to give themselves the best chance at the Olympics. 'These guys are following a very regimented, professional line. This is a new breed, a new generation of Irish people – confident, capable, intelligent, high achieving.'

One of those high achievers is Joanne Cuddihy, who smashed the eight-year-old Irish 400 m record at the World Championships in Osaka. Finishing in a time of 50.73 seconds to take fourth place in her semi-final, she beat Karen Shinkins' record of 51.07, set in 1999. Joanne just missed out on qualifying for the world final, but her performance in Osaka helped her make some hard decisions.

'I knew from the summer that I had to go for it. Loughborough was the obvious choice. I probably should have come earlier,' admits the Kilkenny woman, who had previously tried training in Canada and California for short periods, and turned down the offer of an athletics scholarship to Harvard University. 'The US route had gone sour for me. It was such a culture shock.'

Loughborough's world-class facilities were a big attraction, she says. At the university, she has access to a heated indoor track, an enormous gym and an elite weights room. And, best of all, she can walk from one to the other. With the traffic in Dublin, she recalls, it could take her two buses – and two hours – to go between the UCD gym and the track at Santry. 'There were so many things I put up with that I wouldn't allow now,' she recalls.

Nick Dakin, Loughborough's Director of Coaching, says he thinks the key thing the university has to offer is the right environment. 'It's a pretty compact centre, the athletes don't have to walk too far from the track to the gym, to massage or physio. You can do four or five different elements in the course of the day without having to spend too much time travelling.' Training to be a successful athlete is never easy, he says, but Loughborough makes it 'as easy as it's possible to be'.

Martyn Rooney, a top British 400 m runner who is also a member of Nick Dakin's training group, says Loughborough is a proven athletics hothouse. 'You look at the past – Seb Coe, Paula Radcliffe, Dave Moorcroft – Olympic champions, world record holders – they all came here. Loughborough has past success. And Nick has had consistently good groups.'

The Irish athletes, says Rooney, have added greatly to the training group: 'When I first came here I was always at the front of the group. Gillick came along and now I have someone to run with and to chase – and that is awesome, something I didn't have before.'

For Paul Hession, the main reason for moving abroad was the opportunity to work with a world-class coach. 'In April 2005, I was training in Dublin, training hard, training well, but I just felt that if I wanted to be truly world class, I needed something different. And I just didn't see that person in this country. I just don't think they existed, at that time. So I had to go abroad.' Based at Glenrothes, in Fife, about forty-five minutes from Edinburgh, he lives and trains out of the home of the well-known sprint coach Stuart Hogg. 'It was for him I went, absolutely – his ideals and the way he goes about his business, how unbelievably meticulous he is, his unbelievable attention to detail. I just liked the way he trained as well. He's the type of guy who keeps a small, select group of athletes so he can devote a lot of time to each one individually. People disregard how important that is. It's important to have a good group of training partners, fair enough, but it's even more important to get one-on-one time with your coach, and as a result he can make important decisions that will possibly lead to, for example, staying injury free.'

Hogg's group offers high-quality, high-intensity training. Sessions are carefully planned, broken down into the various components of sprinting: speed, speed endurance and strength endurance. It is quite different from what Hession was used to in Ireland where training sessions were often, to use his own words, 'too sloggy'.

He explains: 'In Ireland, for example, people ignore speed endurance – which is the basis of all sprinting. We focus too much on hard training. In this country, if you're not on your back after training, then you haven't trained. In Edinburgh, we focus on quality, and we're able to go and train at high intensity the next day. Instead of doing eight or nine 200s straight through, we break them into sets and we'll have longer recovery.

'And the way we structure our training as well – everything is so planned, it's all on a gradual curve. My experience of training in Ireland is that people train at one level for four-week blocks, and then try to get to another level. Whereas we try to build it up gradually – every day is a progression on the day before.'

Still young, and improving, Hession is the first Irishman to be ranked in the World's Top 20 in the 200 m in the IAAF end-of-year rankings, thanks to his national record of 20.30 seconds.

Also rising up the world rankings are Ireland's three main male walkers – Robert Heffernan, Jamie Costin and Colin Griffin – all of whom are now guided by top foreign coaches.

'There are some very good coaches in Ireland. But there is a difference between being a very good coach and the coach of an Olympic champion,' says 50 km specialist Jamie Costin from Waterford, now coached by Russian Ilya Markov, the former World and European champion, and an Olympic silver medallist.

Costin and Markov are part of an international training group overseen by Robert Korzeniowski, four times an Olympic champion and the first man to win both the 20 km and 50 km walks in the same Olympic competition. The man nicknamed 'The Walking Wizard' is also the personal coach to Rob Heffernan and to Francisco 'Paquillo' Fernández, the Spaniard who won silver at 20 km at both the Athens Olympics and the 2007 World Championships.

'We sourced the best men for the job,' says Jamie Costin, pointing out that Korzeniowski and Markov have 'proven track records', not just as competitors, but as coaches as well.

Rob Heffernan agrees, adding that the Irish are fortunate to have such international expertise in their corner. 'I wrote to Korzeniowski in 2001 and told him how much I admired him,' the Cork man recalls. 'I had a picture taken with him at the closing ceremony in Sydney, where he

Kilkenny sprinter Joanne
Cuddihy — moved to the UK.
(*Sportsfile/Brendan Moran*)

won two golds – he was eight minutes ahead of me in the twenty kilometres. He is an animal.'

On Valentine's Day 2001, the phone rang. It was Korzeniowski. 'I thought it was Pierse O'Callaghan [former Irish international race walker] winding me up. He invited me to go to South Africa to train. My coach Mick Lane started laughing, he wouldn't believe me.'

It was Heffernan's first time to train at altitude, and he stayed for a month. The group worked hard, none harder than Korzeniowski, and Heffernan suffered. 'The first week I did eighty miles, the second week one hundred and twelve. He used to come into the bedroom and laugh at us.'

Korzeniowski has done well from athletics. He has a high position in Polish TV, and is paid a reputed €80,000 a year by the Spanish authorities to coach Fernández. But his interest in Heffernan appears genuinely altruistic, and extends to inviting the Irishman to stay in his home in Poland. And Heffernan is not slow to acknowledge his good fortune. 'I am very lucky that Robert has taken me under his wing,' he says.

In the months leading up to Beijing, Heffernan and Costin have been criss-crossing the world, training or competing in such diverse locations as Spain, South Africa, Poland and Russia. 'I'll be in Ireland for just ten days between March and June,' laughs Costin, who trains twice a day and averages just one day off a fortnight.

Heffernan, who has a little daughter, Meghan, tries to get home to Cork as often as possible. 'If I'm away too long I'm miserable. It's very important to be happy.'

These are real issues, of course, for athletes who move overseas to train. 'I live in England now and I don't like it,' admits Derval O'Rourke. 'But I know I have to suck it up. You need to do everything you can. And then, when you walk away at the end of your career, you won't have any sleepless nights.'

The UK, she says, offers athletes elite coaching and world-class facilities. In Bath, she has daily access to a 150 m indoor heated track. 'In Santry, I'd be training in a hat and gloves. You can only go so far in Ireland. You drag yourself to a point, but you cannot maintain it. We have a major problem with elite coaching. I didn't feel I could run 12.50 here.'

David Gillick, meanwhile, freely admits that there have been times in the unfamiliar territory when he is lonely, even fearful. Often he envies friends who have finished college, moved into jobs and started making real money. 'The truth is, I have wondered sometimes if I was doing the right thing. It was really, really hard leaving Dublin. It's easy at home – you don't think about it, about things like where will I eat, where am I going to live, finances etc. And there are days when I just feel low, days when I just don't want to be in England. All my close friends and family are in Dublin. I was leaving a place I had lived all my life, and basically I didn't know when I'd be back. Deep down, I was scared!

'But the difference here is that every night, when I get into bed, I know I've done a good day's work – I make sure of that. Every athlete, to get to the top, has to make some hard decisions, and certain sacrifices. But I realised deep down what I want.

'That's why I went mental when I won gold in Birmingham. It wasn't just because I won the European Indoor title, but because of everything that had happened over the past year. Winning the gold medal was fantastic, and getting the qualifying standard for the Olympics, and for the World Championships, that was really great. But for me, the main thing was that I proved to myself that I'd made the right decision moving to England last year, and taking on a new coach. After the European Indoors, I knew I was on the right track. I went away from the Europeans knowing that the move to England was the right move.'

Other Irish Olympic contenders training abroad include swimmers Andrew Bree from County Down and Dubliner Barry Murphy, both based at the University of Tennessee in America. Cyclist Nicholas Roche, meanwhile, lives in France and has been training in Malaysia and the Ivory Coast.

Athlete Paul McKee and track cyclist David O'Loughlin have been training in South Africa. Martin Fagan, from Mullingar, on course to be the first Irishman since 1992 to compete in an Olympic marathon, is a former scholarship student at Providence College, but made the Beijing qualifying standard at the Dubai Marathon in January 2008, after visa difficulties denied him re-entry to America.

Canoeist Eoin Rheinisch has spent months out of the country, training on some of the world's best slalom facilities in Australia, the US and China. He has no choice, he says, as Ireland has no white-water courses. 'I can't understand how an economy like Ireland does not have these facilities,' he says, pointing out that this is, after all, a sport at which Ireland has a tradition of success. Irish boats have qualified for the slalom event at the ten Olympics since the sport was first introduced in 1972. Our best result came in 1996 in Atlanta, when Ian Wiley finished fifth, just out of the medals. 'In France and Germany, these courses are ten to the dozen,' says Rheinisch. 'The Sydney course for the Olympics in 2000 was built for around three million euro – the stadium, the pumps, channels, everything – and it's still in use every single day, with tourists and local people rafting on it. These courses make money.' Poulaphuca or Leixlip Dam, he says, would be ideal locations for such a course in Ireland – 'anywhere there is a steep gradient'.

Ireland's rowing squads, meanwhile, are training in continental Europe – the lightweight crews in Spain, the heavyweights in France. 'In Olympic year we are out of the country for three out of every four weeks,' confirms Mike Heskin, Irish Rowing's International Team Manager. 'We have to spend a considerable amount of time in climate camps, to perfect our technique. In Ireland, our biggest enemy is wind, not rain.'

Olympic triathlon hopeful Gavin Noble from Enniskillen, County Fermanagh, has a permanent base in Scotland, having attended Stirling University on a sports scholarship. He stayed on when Stirling was chosen in 2002 as the headquarters for the Scottish Institute of Sport, who were followed there by Triathlon Scotland. 'Sometimes Ireland is maybe a year behind Britain in terms of development in sport,' says Noble. 'The programmes the British initiate usually come first, and then Ireland follows.' Stirling, he says, is the perfect base, as he can join in with the Scots on their programme, use the campus facilities, including the 50 m pool, and enjoy a varied training terrain. He also travels widely, training and racing in Spain in the early weeks of 2008, and spending no fewer than thirty-five weeks abroad in 2007. In a bid to become the first Irish triathlete to qualify for the Olympics, he has been travelling the world in search of points, competing in up to fifteen races a year, most of them overseas. At one stage in late 2006, he did three events on three different continents in a ten-day period. Now firmly ensconced inside the Top 10 in the International Triathlon Union's European Cup rankings, he was competing for the last European place in the Olympics with two Hungarians, two Dutch, a Croatian and a Greek.

Ireland's top two shooters, Derek Burnett and Philip Murphy, also spend a great deal of time abroad. The Irish climate, they say, particularly the dark, windy months, plays havoc with this most precise of sports. 'The thing that can let us down here is the weather. It's an outdoor sport and wind is a disaster, because wind can affect the flight line of the target,' explains Burnett, on course for his third Olympic competition. In 2004, in the lead-up to the Athens Olympics, Burnett was out of the country twenty-one times on shooting trips lasting from three days to two weeks. 'I could apply to be a tax exile,' he laughs.

The team's main overseas base is in Italy, where High Performance Director Kevin Kilty has a house. 'Italy has perfect light, and they have shooting ranges like we have GAA pitches – every

Left to right:
Scott Evans (right) with Danish coach Jim Laugesen, former World No. 1; Chloe Magee, from Donegal, trains in Sweden. 'Anyone who wants to be good at badminton needs to move away from Ireland.'
(*Ed Smyth*)

twenty miles you run into one,' says Burnett. In the winter, the shooters also travel regularly to Kuwait, where they can get in up to ten rounds of practice each day, some 250 shots. They base themselves at the range built for the Asian Shooting Championships – at a cost of $28 million. When they were leaving, in January, the sheikh who runs the resort came out to thank them for coming. 'He told us we would see many improvements the next time we came, that they were going to spend a further two million dollars finishing the facilities,' recalls Burnett, reeling from the figures. 'Two million, to finish! If only we had two million for facilities in Ireland.'

In badminton, a sport which thrives in Asia and Scandinavia, it is no surprise to learn that Ireland's two leading hopefuls for 2012 are both living and training overseas. Chloe Magee from Donegal is in Sweden, working with top coach Tommy Reidy from Limerick, who represented USA in the Barcelona Olympics in 1992. Dubliner Scott Evans is based in Denmark.

'At the moment, I don't think Ireland has the facilities or the coaches to allow players to train full-time for badminton,' says Chloe Magee. 'Anyone who wants to be good at badminton needs to move away from Ireland.'

Scott Evans, who became the No. 1 player in Ireland at just sixteen years of age, agrees. 'You need to train with better players, play against people who are better than you. Also, I need a full-time coach, someone I can work with four or five hours a day. So, for me, the move to Denmark just had to be done.'

In Denmark, Evans is coached by Jim Laugesen, himself an Olympian and a former World No. 1 in Doubles. He says the Irishman is 'a skilled player, with huge potential', and admits 'the Olympics is the big goal' for both of them.

Denmark's club system, its tournament play, and the sheer number of players make it an excellent choice for players looking for top-class training. 'The set-up over there is just perfect,' says Scott. 'They have everything that needs to be there for badminton.'

Under the Dane's tutelage, the Dubliner has made significant progress, with his 2007 highlights including wins over former World No. 1, Lee Hyun Il of Korea and World No. 15 Shoji Sato (Japan). In April 2008, he became the first Irish player ever to reach the quarter-finals of the European Singles Championships, beating high-ranked players from Bulgaria, Germany and Russia, before losing in two tight sets to the No.1 seed, Denmark's Kenneth Jonassen, the World No. 5 who once held the record for the fastest smash in the world: 298 km/h (185 mph).

Evans, whose current world ranking is in the low forties, says that his move overseas, at the age of seventeen, was the right one – but personally difficult. 'Leaving friends and family is hard. I couldn't finish school, either. It's tough.'

College Prospects of America (CPOA), an international agency that finds places for promising talent, estimates that well over 100 Irish youngsters every year take scholarships to US colleges. 'They are mainly track and field athletes, golfers, and a few tennis and hockey players,' says Marva Hall, of CPOA, who can number big names like Luke Donald (Golf, Northwestern University) and Karen Stupples (Golf, Florida State University) among her clients. 'Quite a lot of Northern Ireland kids go for soccer.'

Scholarship packages can be worth up to $200,000, offering students four years of paid tuition leading to a degree, plus living and sporting expenses. Student athletes are never paid, but get free accommodation, food, travel, professional coaching and equipment, and the opportunity to develop their skills in a highly competitive system. 'It's the nearest thing that amateur athletes can get to a pro circuit,' says Marva Hall, who says the top sporting and academic college is Stanford University in California. 'It is Oxbridge standard, every bit as academic as Harvard, and every year they win the overall award for the most collegiate sporting titles.'

The student athletes' ambitions, says Hall, vary widely. Most of the golfers and tennis players are hoping to play professionally. Those who go to play hockey know that they are unlikely to make any money from sport. Runners, meanwhile, and swimmers, know that they will get four years of fierce competition and that they are following the same path as Olympic medallists of the past. According to Hall, practically every British swimming gold medallist from the 1960s to the present day has been produced with the help of the US college system. Hall estimates that some 70 per cent of student athletes stay for the full four years, and find that the experience makes them 'very marketable' in their future lives. A small number of golfers have gone on to play pro, but very few tennis players.

The flight overseas, however, is nothing new. Great Irish athletes of the past, including Ronnie

Delany, John Treacy and Eamonn Coghlan, have all gone to America to find the right training and competition.

John Treacy's alma mater is Providence College, Rhode Island. 'It was the thing to do then,' he recalls. 'You went out to America, to college, to train. It was probably the best decision I ever made, in that I went to a college that didn't over-race me, and I was training with a group of guys that, in essence, helped me to develop my talent. It worked out extremely well for me.'

Indeed it did. Following four years of great collegiate success in America, including several National Collegiate Athletic Association (NCAA) titles, he exploded onto the world stage in 1978, becoming the first Irishman to win the IAAF World Cross Country Championship. He repeated the triumph the following year in front of a home crowd.

He returned to Ireland in 1980 and learned how difficult it was to work and train at the same time. 'I fell flat on my face,' he admits. Feeling he was wasting his talent and his time, he decided to return with America, even though it meant uprooting his new family – wife Fionnuala, and their first child, Caoimhe. 'We went out in 1983 for a year, to Rhode Island – and stayed for eleven.'

The USA offered him a training environment, high-level training partners – 'guys to train with, that train at a very high level, along with yourself, more people at your level'. In Dublin, he recalls, he would usually be forced to lead every training run, to make sure he got the pace he needed. In Rhode Island, running with a dozen high-class athletes, he could share the workload.

The better weather, he admits, was also 'a huge factor'. Every year, come 1 January, he moved to Phoenix, Arizona, for two and a half months of warm-weather training. 'If you're on a track running in shorts and T-shirt, that environment lends itself to training at a good level, you're not dodging wind, snow, rain. You wake up the next day and you're certain of the weather.' Crucially, he adds, the warmer weather helps to avoid injuries.

There's a price to be paid, of course. 'There were times when I wouldn't have spoken to anyone during the course of the day, only on the phone – that's a lonely existence.' But it paid off, spectacularly, with a silver medal at the Los Angeles Olympics in 1984 – his first ever marathon. It was Ireland's first track medal since Ronnie Delany won gold in Melbourne in 1956.

To this day, Providence College retains strong Irish links. John Treacy's brother, Ray, is the Director of Cross Country and Track Operations, and the Rhode Island university can count current Olympic contenders Mary Cullen, Martin Fagan, and Róisín McGettigan among its alumni. McGettigan, from Wicklow, explains why she took the decision to go west: 'Back in 1999, when I did the Leaving Cert, as an athlete you could go to Limerick or UCD, but there was no distance programme in Limerick and no system in UCD. I knew I was getting to that point where I had to up my training. I wanted teammates, and not to feel abnormal by going out training. I was thinking about going to the UK.'

When McGettigan was in sixth year, Ray Treacy came to Wicklow to visit her. He showed her a list of athletes who had gone to Providence, their race times when they started and the improvements they made while at college. He offered her a four-year scholarship, an education worth over $100,000, with everything covered: gear, medical backup, coaching, travel. 'I jumped at the chance,' recalls the steeplechaser. 'I could not wait to go.'

She was desperately homesick during her freshman year – an experience shared by many Irish scholarship athletes, who are often surprised by the very real cultural differences. 'I came over with a friend from Limerick. We were shell-shocked, but we had each other to cry with. I do not think I would have survived without her.'

Over time, McGettigan settled in. 'It worked for me,' she says. 'It was great to be part of something that was a nationally recognised, established programme. I bought into the system. You get four years to develop, there's a plan . . . you do the big meets, cross country, indoors, outdoors, you learn how to travel a lot.'

McGettigan made good use of her time, majoring in psychology and adding a Masters in Educational Counselling. As an athlete, she also improved every year, finishing her varsity career at No. 3 overall in the US college steeplechase rankings. By that stage, she says, she was ready to be very competitive at international level.

'If I'd stayed in Ireland, I would have been competing against a handful of girls – there is such a small group of athletes at home when you get to that age. In Providence, I was in a team with twenty or thirty girls and boys, all around the same age, all training every day.' McGettigan is fulsome, too, in her praise of Ray Treacy, who is still coaching her, Mary Cullen and Martin Fagan, even though they have all graduated. 'Ray has so much experience. I don't think he's ever had someone go home,' she laughs. 'And I haven't bought a pair of shoes since I left Ireland in 1999.'

US scholarships, of course, do not suit everyone. Alistair Cragg, who went on scholarship to Southern Methodist University in Texas, says his first experiences of college life were 'bad'. He was homesick, he had left a girlfriend behind, and he did not get on with the SMU coach. 'It felt like the coach was using me, which was me not trusting him. It never worked.' He quit college and stopped running for several months. His brother, meanwhile, contacted all the major running colleges, and the University of Arkansas – where the head coach is Mayo man John McDonnell – came in for him. Now, after a glittering college career, where he won multiple NCAA titles, he says he still identifies with every youngster who's struggled in America. 'It's tough, especially at eighteen, nineteen.' And he praises McDonnell, who is still his coach, for helping him get through. 'I know there's a lot of kids who go over there, and it hasn't worked out,' he says. 'I think with athletes going there, if they're going there with the right intentions, to get an education, and to trust somebody, then it will work. But if someone goes over there with a little bit of doubt, they're just going to fail.' Scholarships, he says, are a good way to develop as an athlete, in a protected environment. 'I recommend it. It's a great chance to become somebody and get your goals in life. You forget what it's like to be a kid. Responsibility just comes on to your shoulders. If you're ready for it, it's a dream. It's like a bridge you have to cross in your life and it's a way to get pushed across it.' To succeed abroad, however, he maintains that home support is crucial. 'For a kid that's leaving their friends and their family and eating different food and driving on the wrong side of the road . . . to be told at home that it's not going to work, I know it wouldn't have worked for me.'

Paul Hession, too, feels he would not have done as well, had he taken the option of an American scholarship. 'I don't think it would have been the right option for me. Being a late developer – coming out of school I was skinny, underdeveloped – that would have been a recipe for disaster going into a tough collegiate system. I needed a long-term plan, and that's not the case in the States. They want results. They don't care what state you're in leaving college, they only care what sort of state you're in *in* college.'

For those who do not want to cross the water, today's athletes have a widening range of choices. Leaving school, Derval O'Rourke turned down American offers, fearing that she would be swallowed up by the collegiate factory system, and took a scholarship to UCD instead. Fionnuala

Britton, from the same club and county as Róisín McGettigan, was also offered a Providence College scholarship, but she turned it down. Four years behind Róisín, she did not like the idea of moving so far away from home or changing coach – and she had the option of a sports scholarship to Dublin City University.

'DCU has everything I need,' she says. 'I can live and train here and go to college.' Now studying for a Masters degree, she lives rent-free in an accommodation block with fifty other athletes, a mix of men and women. There are five floors, two apartments per floor, each with five en suite bedrooms. 'It's working. I'm not going to change something that is not broken,' says the Slí Cualann runner who won silver in the Under-23 European Cross Country Championships in 2006, then qualified for the 3,000 m steeplechase final at the Worlds in Osaka. At DCU, top-class athletes have the luxury of access to a separate elite gym – 'So you're not trying to compete with people to get on a treadmill.' Academically, too, says Britton, the lecturers are understanding about the demands on elite athletes – 'there is a bit of leeway'.

DCU's sports scholarships, first introduced in 1996, now benefit in excess of 100 young athletes each year, across a broad range of sports including athletics, basketball, boxing, camogie, canoeing, Gaelic football, golf, handball, hockey, hurling, rugby, rowing, sailing, soccer and tennis. Depending on an athlete's achievements, potential and needs, the college's Elite Athlete Development Programme also offers support services which may include financial assistance with academic fees, equipment, books, travel to competitions, accommodation on campus, athlete career education workshops, membership to the University Sports Club, access to the Elite Performance Gym, goal setting and performance planning, sports injury management, sports psychology, nutritional advice and fitness testing.

Among those to have taken DCU scholarships in recent times are top athletes Ailis McSweeney and David Campbell, senior footballers Kevin Reilly, Bryan Cullen, Stephen Cluxton and Conor Mortimer and boxer Darren Sutherland.

Studying for a BSc in Sports Science and Health, Sutherland secured his Olympic place at the final qualifying tournament in April – and returned to face exams in May, after missing nearly three months of classes. He is sanguine, however, about his double life. 'It's a nice break to get away from training and focus on something else.' he says. 'There is a life after boxing. I have ambitions beyond boxing. I want to work in sports science. This is actually my third year in second year. I have been taking a couple of modules each semester, just chipping away at it. I am in no rush to graduate, because I am not going to practise in that field until my boxing is finished.'

Like Fionnuala Britton, Sutherland lives rent-free on campus, and says that is hugely important to him. 'For me to commute from Navan, where my family live, to the national stadium would not have been possible. DCU has been very good to me, very positive and understanding.'

The Easiest Gold Medal

'They don't give you gold medals for beating somebody. They give you gold medals for beating everybody.'

– Michael Johnson, five-time Olympic champion

Of all the Olympic gold medals, which is the easiest to win?

Is it a race, or a contest, a team sport, or an individual event?

Well, Australian scientists think they have the answer . . .

It is sledging – women's skeleton, to be precise, at the Winter Olympics.

That bold assertion comes from physiologists at the Australian Institute of Sport. They have been studying a wide range of sports, looking for events that are 'weak' internationally, that do not attract huge numbers of competitors, and which might be targeted by an ambitious sporting nation. Then, to take maximum advantage, the Australians have developed a system known as 'talent transfer', moving athletes from one sport to another, to find the one best suited to them.

The skeleton – so called because it is, effectively, a stripped-down bobsleigh – involves the slider racing face-first down a mile-long ice tunnel, suffering six times the force of gravity over

Opposite page:
Kirsty McGarry.

Alpine skier Tamsen McGarry carries the Irish flag during the Opening Ceremony of the Salt Lake City Winter Olympic Games 2002. (*Getty Images/Clive Mason*)

two dozen sickening turns. It is one of sport's most terrifying and risk-filled events, and sliders travel at speeds of over 120 km/h (75 mph): the top speed on Irish roads. However, it is hardly a mass participation sport, and therefore the talent pool is relatively shallow. Success in the event is also, crucially, highly dependent on a single sporting attribute – speed.

In fact, up to 50 per cent of the success in the skeleton is based on start speed – those thirty metres at the start of the race where the slider sprints off, getting up as much speed as possible, before throwing herself on to the sled.

Scientists have discovered an unusually high correlation between how quickly the competitor gets off the mark and how high they will be placed in the race. Beyond the start, as the slider steers the skeleton down the course, there are only a limited number of variables affecting performance.

To test their theory, in 2004 the AIS undertook a national advertisement campaign, inviting women athletes from other sports to try out for the new skeleton squad. Some seventy serious contenders came forward, and around thirty-five likely competitors were selected for a training camp based on their body type, 30 m sprint times and attitude. This was whittled down to a squad of ten, a diverse group, including a World champion water skier and several high-level sprinters. One of them was an eighteen-year-old gymnast and sprinter, Michelle Steele, from Bundaberg on Australia's hot Queensland coast. Her natural habitat was beach and surf, and her only sight of snow had been on a brief school outing to the Snowy Mountains.

'They targeted women they thought would be fast and explosive over thirty metres,' Steele told newspapers at the time. 'I was doing surf lifesaving here, sprinting on the beach. The sports institute put out the word to the surf lifesaving club and I heard about it that way.'

In a bid to cram five to six years of skeleton experience into two years, the women were put through a 'talent transfer' crash course of intensive training and analysis. They prepared for competition on an old sled fitted with skate wheels to replicate the motion of a sled on ice. They practised take-off on a floor-level treadmill, every push charted by the institute's biomechanists, the speeds and force-levels logged by special accelerator devices. They then moved to Calgary, Canada, to train with a top American bobsleigh coach.

They then began to compete.

With just thirteen weeks of on-ice experience behind her, Michelle Steele's first competitive outing was simply sensational. Making her World Cup debut in Calgary in November 2005, she finished in sixth place, recording the fastest push time in the opening heat and the second fastest time in the final heat on the Olympic track.

A few months later, less than two years after swapping sand sprinting for ice, she finished thirteenth at the Winter Olympics in Turin. At the start of 2008, she was ranked No. 8 in the world, a serious medal contender for the 2010 Winter Games.

Flushed with success, the AIS has now turned its attention to other winter sports. Former gymnasts and trampolinists are being taught aerial skiing techniques, surfers and skateboarders are being transformed into snowboarders, and new facilities have been built for aerial skiing and half-pipe snowboarding.

But can they really compete against the traditional winter sports powerhouses – like Austria, Norway and Sweden? Geoff Lipshut, director of Australia's Olympic Winter Institute, had this retort for the traditional opposition: 'The only thing they have is snow and mountains.'

Alisa Camplin, the first Australian to win medals at consecutive Winter Olympics, is another 'talent transfer' success story. The Melbourne aerial skier won gold at the 2002 Salt Lake Winter Games and followed that with bronze at Turin in 2006. But her background is not in winter sports at all – she was a successful junior runner, gymnast and sailor. She saw snow for the first time on a high school trip, took up skiing at nineteen and was twenty-one years old when she first competed as an aerial skier. Never completely at home on the ice, she famously flattened her victory flowers when she fell over in Salt Lake on her way to a news conference. And success at this most perilous of sports has taken its toll – she has suffered injuries including a broken collarbone, broken hand, two broken ankles and nine concussions.

Britain, too, has had some success with transforming sprinters into winter athletes. Shelley Rudman won a skeleton silver medal at the 2006 Winter Olympics, less than four years after transferring from athletics.

It should not be forgotten, of course, that Ireland has also had some small success in winter sports. There has even been an Irish gold medallist – Robin Dixon (bobsleigh, 1964) – although he was competing for Britain.

In more recent times, Ireland narrowly missed out on a medal in the 2002 Winter Olympics in Salt Lake City – when the Galway peer, Lord Clifton Wrottesley, finished in fourth place in the skeleton.

Terry McHugh, meanwhile, has the unique distinction of being the only athlete to represent Ireland at both Summer and Winter Olympics. The Tipperary man, who won twenty-one consecutive national javelin titles from 1984 to 2004, competed in four Summer Olympics, starting in 1988 – and still found time to qualify for two Winter Games, where he represented Ireland in the bobsleigh.

At the most recent Winter Games (Turin, 2006) four first-time Olympians carried Ireland's hopes: Alpine skiers Thos Foley and Kirsty McGarry, cross-country skier Rory Morrish and skeleton racer David Connolly. They joined more than 2,500 athletes, from 75 nations, competing in 15 winter sports.

In Turin, Ireland's best placing was twentieth, again in the skeleton – piloted by 25-year-old Connolly – like Michelle Steele, a sprinter-turned-slider.

The Wicklow man recorded runs of 59.97 seconds and one minute flat on the Cesana Pariol ice track, hitting a top speed of 75 mph. Though he finished nineteen places behind the winner, only four seconds separated Connolly from Canada's Duff Gibson – who, at thirty-nine, became the oldest gold medallist for an individual event in the history of Winter Olympics.

Kirsty McGarry, meanwhile – whose sister, Tamsen, was the first Irish woman to compete in the Winter Games – finished thirty-second in the giant slalom. There was a personal highlight, too, in the slalom, as she posted the best Olympics points score ever by an Irish Alpine ski racer. Though still only in her early twenties, she has amassed more than sixty medals in Fédération Internationale de Ski (FIS) races, has competed at Europa Cup and World Cup, and is the first

Irish skier to achieve Olympic 'A' status in all four major downhill events – Slalom, Giant Slalom, Super G and Super Combined.

'For a non-Alpine nation, Ireland's growing stature in winter sports is remarkable and one in which we have an excellent sporting future,' says Olympic Council of Ireland president Pat Hickey. 'More and more Irish people are taking winter sports holidays and this has fuelled the interest in a major way.'

Stephen Martin, chief executive of the OCI, confirms that there are plans to develop a more diverse squad for the Vancouver Winter Olympics of 2010. He says he is trying to 'change the mindset of the funding agencies', to encourage the development of specific performance programmes for winter sports. It is important, he says, to 'think outside the box', and identify sports in which Ireland might make a quick impact. Martin, from Bangor, who previously worked with

From left to right:
Thos Foley, Olympic skier (*Niall O'Flynn*); Kirsty McGarry, Ireland's leading skier.

the British Olympic Association, says the UK has had great success in some of the more obscure sports. 'Who would have thought eight years ago that British curling would be where they are now? I don't think people in Ireland mind which sport. If they see an Irish athlete up on a podium, they'll say "well done".'

'The OCI has already had preliminary meetings with the Irish Sports Council to develop a strategy for identifying and funding a small focused group of winter athletes,' he says. 'For instance, we hope for Vancouver to add qualifiers in disciplines such as curling, snowboarding, bobsleigh and even ice skating. Our men's curlers are in European Division 'A' with world-class teams, something

Clockwise from top:
The Irish Men's Curling Team – winners of the European 'B' Championships, 2007. From left: Neil Fyfe, Peter J. Wilson, Robin Gray, Peter Wilson, Tony Tierney and Canadian coach Ron Meyers (*Hugh Stewart*); Lord Clifton Wrottesley, finished in fourth place in the skeleton at the 2002 Winter Olympics in Salt Lake City; RTÉ's Shane O'Donoghue (right) with Jim Tibbetts, Ireland coach, on the night Ireland's ice hockey team won the silver medal in Division 3 of the 2007 World Championships, and earned promotion to Division 2 (*Niall O'Flynn*); Bobsleigh team Siobhán and Aoife Hoey. (*Hoey family*)

our men's hockey team would be happy with at present – and the curlers receive no government funding.'

'In Vancouver I think we could be quite strong,' says Pat Hickey, who joins Martin in lobbying for greater funding for winter sports. He is also liaising with the Irish expatriate community in Vancouver to organise training camps for the Irish contenders.

His ambitions are not unrealistic. Ireland's ice hockey team won the silver medal in Division 3 of the 2007 World Championships, and earned promotion to Division 2. In bobsleigh, Ireland already has a history of qualifying a men's team, and had a women's bob in contention for Turin – though Portarlington's Siobhán Hoey, the former national triple-jump champion, and her sister, Aoife, ultimately missed out on qualification.

The Irish men's curling team, meanwhile, is now ranked in Europe's Top 10, following success at the European 'B' Championships in Füssen, Germany, in December of 2007. The Irish team went through the competition undefeated, winning the gold medal and gaining promotion to the elite 'A' Division, alongside the traditional curling superpowers of Scotland, Norway, Denmark, Switzerland and Germany.

Not bad for a nation that doesn't have a curling rink!

'No, we don't have a home,' admits Gordon McIntyre, the President of the Irish Curling Association, which has around fifty members. The Irish squad, however, is largely based in Scotland, where they have access to forty or so excellent rinks. The two Irish-based internationals, Peter Wilson and Robin Gray, travel over regularly to train and compete. The team got together in answer to an advertisement in a curling magazine in the early 1990s, and is part-funded by the OCI, who granted them €14,000 in 2007 to help engage the services of a top Canadian coach. The target now is a place at the Winter Olympics in 2010. Into the future, says Pat Hickey, a medal is not out of the question. 'This is not the most contested medal sport.'

Experts add, however, that if Ireland realistically expects to compete in winter sports, then the winter sports federations need to become more professional. Ireland's Chef de Mission at the Salt Lake Games, Larry Tracey, says that the Irish team, right now, lacks quality coaching, medical assistance and technical backup. Ski and sled technicians are a vital ingredient of any modern team. The USA have simulators to train their bobsleigh teams, the Austrians use wind tunnels to test their skiers.

Larry Tracey believes that, to make any real impact on future Olympic Games, Ireland's skiers would need professional coaching. And that means having a team of five or more Irish driving each other forward. No world-class coach will commit to a single athlete. He points out that some of the old Eastern Bloc countries, such as Croatia, have come through to win medals in slalom. Spain, too, has done it – and that is a country with little record in snow sports.

The Canadians, he says, have offered to help: 'there's a lot of good will towards Ireland'. Some federations have introduced a 'solidarity programme', where top coaches work with developing nations. The people who run winter sports, he says, want the medals to be spread over many countries.

Ireland may also have to accept that a country with little or no pedigree in winter sports might be better off specialising, not in downhill skiing, but in events such as skeleton, bobsleigh, Nordic skiing, speed skating, snowboard and ice skating.

Tracey adds: 'Ireland has a better chance in sports like Nordic skiing. We have a good record in rowing, cycling and middle-distance running, which involve many of the same physical skills as cross-country skiing or speed skating. A number of cyclists have already, in fact, made the successful transfer to win medals in speed skating. The Irish are good dancers – so ice skating might be a worthwhile gamble.'

11

Minority Sports, Major Ambitions

The GAA, clearly, and soccer have the first pick from the nation's talent pool, and have strong systems for participation and development. The rugby schools pick up a lot of promising youngsters, too. But there are encouraging signs that a number of other Irish sporting federations are also working hard to identify and develop young talent. Sailing, hockey and tennis are among the smaller sports with big ambitions . . .

SAILING

It has been nearly three decades since Ireland last won an Olympic sailing medal. That was at the Moscow Games in 1980, when David Wilkins and Jamie Wilkinson took silver in the Flying Dutchman class.

Today, there are about a dozen Irish Olympic contenders competing on a full-time basis plus another half-dozen who are sailing professionally. At the 2008 Games, Ireland will have at least six representatives in four boats. Athens Olympian Ger Owens has qualified again in the 470 class, and is accompanied this time by Phil Lawton. Tim Goodbody will compete in the Finn and Ciara

team coaches, Passmore and Gene Muller, have set up a monitoring system. Players are required to input daily information on their morning heart rate, quality of sleep, muscle soreness and levels of energy and hunger. On the practice field, player heart rates are monitored with chest straps, to see how hard they work, and how fast they recover.

In the near future, hockey can look forward to joining GAA, soccer and rugby as one of the key sports to be facilitated in the initial phase of the development of the Abbotstown Sports Development Complex. Included in the development plans are an international-grade, water-based hockey pitch, accommodation for up to 100 athletes, a full sports science/sports medicine unit and a cardiovascular strength and conditioning unit. 'It potentially provides us with an essential training hub where we can train, technically and tactically, as a team,' says Passmore. Accommodation on site, he says, is a key plus, which will greatly reduce the hotel bills suffered by Irish sports teams at home training camps. 'At the moment, it's cheaper for us to go and train in France for three days than it is to train here.'

TENNIS

Tennis, strangely enough, plays a significant role in Ireland's Olympic history. In fact, tennis supplied the first gold medal ever won by an Irishman. Dubliner John Pius Boland won the tennis singles at the Athens Olympics of 1896, then added a second gold medal partnering Germany's Fritz Traun in the doubles. In an extraordinary twist of fate, Boland, a talented all-rounder, was visiting Athens on a holiday, and was entered into the competition by a Greek friend who thought he showed promise.

Boland, whose medals were for many years wrongly attributed to the UK, has now been given his proper recognition. He went on to become a well-known Irish nationalist politician. In an amusing coincidence, he attended the same Dublin boys' school, CUS (Catholic University School), as Ronnie Delany.

More than a century later, that tennis success has still not been replicated. Currently, Ireland's highest-ranked players are Louk Sorensen, who is ranked around the top 250 in the world, and Conor Niland, who is just outside the top 300. Modern Ireland's most successful tennis Olympian is Owen Casey, who competed in three successive Games: Seoul 1988, Barcelona 1992 and Atlanta 1996.

Into the future, Tennis Ireland is counting on a new residential programme to move Irish players up the world rankings.

At the National Tennis Centre in Dublin City University, children as young as ten live and train like professional players, in the hope of making it to future Wimbledons and US Opens.

'Our goal is to get someone into the top one hundred in the world,' says Garry Cahill, the Technical Director of Tennis Ireland. 'I'd like to think we can achieve that within five or six years.'

Louk Sorensen – Ireland's highest-ranked tennis player. (*Sportsfile/Paul Mohan*)

The DCU centre boasts four top-class indoor courts. A further three clay courts, and three US Open-style concrete courts, are being added, as part of a €1 million development project. Tennis Ireland is also adding cameras and tracking devices, to follow the movement of players and provide three-dimensional technical analysis.

The real innovation, however, is the fact that the players live on site – as they would in the US, or in many European tennis programmes. Four boys and four girls, aged from ten to sixteen, live in DCU accommodation, most of them in a five-bedroomed apartment served by en suite bedrooms, a house lady and a chef.

The children, who come from as far afield as Belfast and Cork, train up to twenty-four hours a week, over six days, and attend local schools. Their parents drop them off on Sunday or Monday and collect them on Friday evenings. The younger ones hit the courts at 6.45 a.m., three mornings a week. A further eight young players come after school, and do physical work on their own.

Cahill is adamant that young tennis players need to do specific technical and physical training between the ages of ten and thirteen. 'If you wait til they're thirteen or fourteen, it's too late. It's almost impossible to catch up.'

The key thing, he says, it to make it fun for the younger kids, so that it is something they enjoy doing. The physical programme, although clearly aimed at giving the players the skills they will need as competitors, is largely based on fun games, and includes a variety of sports, such as table tennis, badminton and soccer.

He admits: 'It's not the norm in Ireland to do this, for young kids to train like professional athletes, but successful countries in tennis have been doing it for a long time.' He instances players like Maria Sharapova, whose penniless father took her to live and train in Florida as an eight-year-old child, leaving her mother behind in Siberia.

Ideally, Cahill would like to see Ireland bite the bullet and set up specialist sports schools – like the Belgian 'Topsport' training schools, where children have reduced school hours, get off school at 12.30 p.m., and then train. 'I think that is fantastic. I would love to see those here.' In the meantime, however, he hopes that the Dublin programme will offer an alternative to the US scholarship system, which has drained Ireland of its best young talent for thirty years. 'The US college system is not the first option for tennis players any more,' he says.

Although the tennis centre opened only in 2005, and residential training did not begin until a year after that, the early results are encouraging. 'Since we have them living here their level has jumped,' says Garry Cahill. The first member of the academy to break into the senior Irish team is Amy Bowtell from Greystones. She made her debut for Ireland's Federation Cup team in early 2008, aged just fourteen, the youngest player ever to represent Ireland in Fed Cup. She has also done exceptionally well in European competition, and should soon break into the world's Top 300 Under-18s. 'She is the real deal,' says Cahill, who doubles as Ireland's Federation Cup captain. 'At fourteen, she is on track. She can be top one hundred in women's tennis, and I have never said that before about any Irish player.'

On the boys' side, Limerick's Sam Barry, who turned sixteen in 2008, has been one of the fastest movers up the International Tennis Federation's Under-18 rankings.

Tennis Ireland's biggest problem, says Cahill, is getting access to a pool of young talent – especially children from outside the relatively rarified world of Irish tennis. Asked what he looks for in a potential athlete, he says he prefers to get them early – as young as six years of age, so they can start a general programme of physical activity. They have to be quick, with fast feet, have some level of co-ordination, and it is important that they show a desire to play tennis. Interestingly, he says, close access to tennis courts can be a key element of success. He thinks rural children often have more of a mental toughness – a vital edge which is displayed on a daily basis by the Russians and East Europeans on the pro tour.

He is adamant, however, that early competition does not necessarily show up the players with the most potential. 'The players who win at Under-12 level are the players who can keep the ball on the court for the longest. The players who win at senior level are the players who have weapons, and who can hit winners.'

He has recently asked Tennis Ireland to employ a tennis talent identification officer. 'It's about getting access to numbers of kids. The GAA gets them before us. One of the key things is to be able to ID from outside tennis.'

He admits, too, that he expects the best results to come from the Irish girls: 'In our regional programmes we have tried to take in more younger girls. You can probably take a girl with less talent than a boy to national level, and do it quite quickly. When a boy reaches fifteen or sixteen, tennis gets very fast, they're serving at over one hundred mph – so reaction speed, agility, becomes critical. In women's tennis, the ball is not travelling as fast at that stage so you can get away with not being quite as good an athlete. It is easier, too, to make it in women's tennis. If you look at the level of ladies' tennis internationally, it has not progressed at the same speed as the men's.'

One problem for small nations, he says, is the limited number of practice partners for the top men. That does not affect women to the same extent – because a very good woman can practise with the men. 'If you have a very good girl at sixteen or seventeen, she is always going to have sparring partners, even if they are men. A Irish Davis Cup player like Luke Sorensen or Conor Niland would beat a top one hundred woman for sure, maybe even some of the top ten.'

The New Irish

Worldwide, more than seventy million people claim Irish descent. Up to forty-four million Americans claim some Irish blood, as do seven million Australians and six million British residents.

Among them, let us presume, must be quite a few talented athletes. Unfortunately, very few choose to declare for Ireland.

Mary Robinson realised the importance of the Irish 'diaspora'. So did Jack Charlton and the FAI – who built Ireland's most successful soccer team by ruthlessly working the 'granny rule', bringing in players like Andy Townsend, Ray Houghton and John Aldridge.

These players were the children or grandchildren of Irish emigrants, men and women who had left Ireland in poorer times to find a better life. But Ireland has changed and this is now a country that people come to, rather than leave. According to the 2006 Census, the Irish population increased by 322,645 – or 8.2 per cent – between 2002 and 2006. A 2008 report by NCB Stockbrokers found almost 60 per cent of that population increase came from migration, including 'a large influx of persons from the EU accession countries' (ten new countries – the Czech Republic, Cyprus, Estonia, Hungary, Latvia, Lithuania, Malta, Poland, Slovakia and Slovenia – joined the European Union on 1 May 2004.) In 2006 alone, according to NCB, there were 139,000 arrivals from accession

Opposite page:
Experts predict that, in future Games, up to 40 per cent of the Irish team could be made up of people from immigrant backgrounds.

Alistair Cragg (683) competing in the men's 5,000 m in Osaka, Japan. (*Sportsfile/Brendan Moran*)

A Price to be Paid

'A lifetime of training for just ten seconds!'

– Jesse Owens, American Olympic sprinting gold medalist.

As he approached his ninetieth birthday, Britain's great wartime prime minister, Winston Churchill, was once asked the secret of how he had managed to live so long and do so much. 'Sport,' he replied – and the fact that he had never had anything to do with it.

His words, ironically, resonate with many top-class athletes who, despite success on the international stage, worry that their dedication to sport is damaging their future careers and affecting their long-term earning potential.

In fact, a new study indicates that significant numbers of elite Irish athletes believe that their involvement in sport has been bad both for their careers and for their education.

The 2007/2008 study, commissioned by the Irish Institute of Sport and led by Professor Aidan Moran and Dr Suzanne Guerin of University College Dublin, surveyed hundreds of Ireland's elite and recently retired athletes, with a view to identifying the barriers that athletes face during their sporting careers.

Opposite page:
Derval O'Rourke on her way to winning the 60 m hurdles at the World Indoor Championships 2006, Moscow.
(*Sportsfile/Mark Shearman*)

The final survey database, consisting of completed surveys from around a hundred Irish athletes, indicated that a massive 64 per cent have experienced problems taking up job opportunities as a result of their sporting commitments. In addition, although the vast majority of the athletes who responded have a post Leaving Certificate qualification, or are pursuing further study, 28 per cent admitted that their involvement in sport has affected their education in some way.

Linda Caulfield, the former Irish hockey captain, says she is 'not surprised' by the findings of the UCD study. There are particular problems for part-time Irish athletes, she says. 'In Ireland, hockey is amateur. But in many countries across the world, it's semi-professional. The challenge for us is to try to put in the hours of training that the semi-professionals do.'

So why do they do it? 'It's just a fantastic feeling when you have that day when everything goes right for you,' says Caulfield, who admits that the good days are 'few and far between'.

After fourteen years at elite level, the Irish captain decided to step down from the international squad, citing the problems of juggling family, work and training pressures. 'I am in a job now where I have certain commitments and responsibilities. That is one of the reasons why I had to retire.' She is the latest in a long line of international hockey players to step down at their peak, including Sandra O'Gorman, who retired soon after being named as the top goalkeeper at a World Cup, and the former Irish vice-captain, Jenny Burke. Former Irish captain Sarah Kelleher and attacking midfielder Catriona Carey both also retired in their twenties.

Carey stepped down after eight years as an international, earning seventy-two caps. She told *The Irish Times* in 2006 that it was 'a very hard personal decision'. Work pressures, she said, were the main reason for her retirement, plus the fact that she lived so far from the regional and national training sessions. It is a complaint that her brother, Kilkenny hurling star D. J. Carey, and many other GAA county players would understand.

Joanne Cuddihy, the first and only Irish woman ever to break 51 seconds for 400 m, says it is just not possible to work full-time at sport and full-time at a career. 'You cannot have two separate lives.' A final year medical student at UCD, she is training full-time in the run-up to the Olympics, and has had to shelve, for the moment at least, her plans to be a doctor.

The Kilkenny sprinter, who reached the semi-finals of the World Championships in Osaka, recalls how, trying to juggle two high-pressure vocations, she could not give her studies her full attention because of all the training. 'My shortcomings were highlighted every morning on ward round. I couldn't read enough at night.' Conversely, her work as a hospital intern was starting to impact on her body. 'I had 7 a.m. ward rounds. My right knee started to swell up from standing all day in theatre. I was on my feet the whole time, suffering sleep deprivation and stress.'

Eileen O'Keeffe understands how she feels. As a theatre nurse, in Beaumont Hospital, she

Ireland's Cathy McKean (12) is congratulated by team-mates, from left, Eimear Cregan, Linda Caulfield and Jenny McDonough after scoring Ireland's first goal at the 2007 EuroHockey Nations Championships. (*Sportsfile/Pat Murphy*)

worked from 8 a.m. to 4.30 p.m., and did her share on call as well. 'I was out on my feet, coming home from shifts, trying to train – it really wasn't realistic,' says the seven-time Irish hammer throw champion. 'I was doing two training sessions a day on days off and one on work days.' In January 2007, she moved to a three-day week and, in June, became a full-time athlete. Three months later, at the World Athletics Championships, she finished sixth. But she is glad, she says, that she kept her dual focus for as long as she did.

'I wanted to get my qualification, theatre nurse, and I knew if I didn't do it then, I would never go back. Now I feel I have my job there to go back to when I want to. I have a permanent post in Beaumont. I'm qualified in the area that I love. I have no regrets now if the athletics doesn't work out I have a job that I want to go back to there. I don't lose either way.'

Most athletes agree that, before things get too serious, study and training, or work and training can benefit each other. It gets more difficult, however, as you progress in sport or career. UCD, says Joanne Cuddihy, has been very accommodating, allowing her to break up her studies, but hospitals, not unreasonably, do not accept the Olympics as an excuse. Add to that the two knee operations, one on the right, one on the left, that she underwent in 2005, plus a bout of glandular fever, and it is no surprise that she considered early retirement from athletics. 'At the end of 2005, I was very close to giving up. I probably would have packed it in, but I decided to give it one year and just go for it.' She knew, she says, that she could run under 51 seconds, but she did not expect the 'dream year' that was 2006, where she achieved Olympic 'A' qualifying standard, ran personal

Left to right:
Eileen O'Keeffe, juggling nursing and athletics; Sprinter Joanne Cuddihy – 'You cannot have two separate lives.'
(*Sportsfile/Brendan Moran*)

bests in the 200 m and 400 m, breaking the long-standing Irish 400 m record in the latter.

Now living and training in the UK, at Loughborough University, she has left behind her home, her studies and her boyfriend. 'It was very tough,' she admits. She is expected back to do obstetrics 'the minute I finish in Beijing', and still hopes to qualify as a doctor in the summer of 2009. 'I have come too far in Medicine to drop it,' she says. 'The year after the Olympics is a down year. Probably I will work for a year in an internship.' But she will not be giving up her athletic career. 'At this point I intend to be in London in 2012.'

Paul Hession, like Cuddihy, is expected to be back at medical college in September. He is now on his second sabbatical from NUI Galway, and is training in Scotland with world-class sprint coach Stuart Hogg. Were it not for athletics, he would have qualified as a doctor in the summer of 2006. But he has no doubts that he has chosen the right path. 'Put it this way – I'm very happy with what I'm doing. At the moment. I've had the best year of my life, I can say that without any hesitation. I'd find it hard at the moment to back down on what I'm doing. Because once you've committed as much as I have, and you've seen results, it's hard then to take your foot off the pedal when you think you can get more. We'll see. My girlfriend always says she can't see me being a doctor until 2014 – until after London. She jokingly says that, but I think part of her believes it.'

Left to right:
Walker Jamie Costin – 'People don't see sport as a job. It's seen as a hobby.' (*Sportsfile/Brendan Moran*); Scott Evans – made the hard decision to leave school before sitting his Leaving Certificate. (*Ed Smyth*)

Many athletes, of course, have no option but to juggle training with other responsibilities, especially if their funding is at the lower levels. Walker Jamie Costin is on a grant of €12,000, and also gets some small sponsorship money. To make ends meet, he does accounts and computer work for the family business and has just qualified as a massage therapist. 'In this country, many people don't see sport as a job. It's seen as a hobby,' he says. 'I was brought up on a farm, and training was something you did before or after work. There was no such thing as rest and recovery.' He plans to stay in the sport up until the London Olympics, but will not make a final decision until after Beijing. There are serious financial considerations, he says, to committing four more years to the Olympic dream. 'I'm thirty-one now. A lot of my friends are settling down, looking to buy houses, getting married. I meet people when I'm home and they ask the question with a bit of hesitation – "Still walking?". You can't build a business or a career while you're involved in sport. There'll be some serious stocktaking done after Beijing.'

Ireland's shooting Olympian, Derek Burnett, runs his own wholesale business, supplying shooting accessories, targets and ammunition. Ireland competes well on the international circuit, he says, but the team's biggest problem is that its international rivals are all full-time shooters. Being self-employed, he has the freedom to travel abroad for competitions and training camps, then work hard when he is at home to keep the business ticking over. 'For me, being away is the closest I can get to being a full-time athlete. When I am away, I am full-time. I'm not worrying about the business,' says the Longford marksman. His teammates, however, do not have the same flexibility. 'We have carpenters, builders, people working in offices. They cannot afford the time to go away.'

The Irish Institute of Sport says the fact that athletes are worrying about careers and studies puts them at a 'competitive disadvantage'. To help address the issue, the institute is running a pilot career development programme, giving twelve athletes the opportunity to work with the recruitment company, Top People. Phil Moore, the Director of Athlete Services for the institute, says the new programme will allow athletes to receive expert career guidance and support. 'It's our belief that high-achieving athletes will become high-achieving workers and we are responding to a critical need. We also believe that this will have a direct impact on performance as each athlete can now remove a stress point from their lives and focus on preparation and competition.'

As far as education is concerned, the system appears to militate against part-time students particularly because, although Irish universities offer free fees for undergraduate students, private colleges and part-time courses charge substantial fees. And even under the free fees scheme, students who have to repeat a year or try to do their degree over a longer period will have to pay repeat fees, often in the region of €6,000 per year. This is a substantial financial penalty for the Irish athlete who chooses to study part-time, says Phil Moore. 'In our competitor nations it's routine for elite athletes to be on "slow-track" education programmes that allow them to fully commit to their training and competition schedules. It's not a level playing field and this is significant barrier to Irish athletes achieving their potential.'

In certain sports, especially the early-specialisation sports, the problem is even more acute. Scott Evans, Irish badminton's leading contender, made the hard decision to leave school before sitting his Leaving Certificate. Ben Lynch, one of our young sailors, has done the same. Boxer John Joe Nevin completed just one year of secondary school.

Garry Cahill, the Technical Director of Tennis Ireland, confirms that the days of gentleman players are over. 'There is no way you are going to be a doctor and a tennis player. It's not possible,'

Fionnula Britton – studying for a Masters.
(*Sportsfile/Brendan Moran*)

he says. He would like to see the school system do more to help school-going athletes, perhaps by offering a three-year Leaving Certificate cycle, as an alternative to Transition Year.

Rory Fitzpatrick, the Irish Sailing Association's Youth & Development Manager and himself an Athens Olympian, tells a similar story: 'The Leaving Cert comes at probably the most important time in a young sailor's life,' he says. At seventeen and eighteen, young sailors are maturing and have the best chance of winning medals in the Youth World Championships, the biggest event in youth sailing, and a predictor of success for the future. The ISA High Performance managers regularly visit school principals and parents to explain the pressures on the sailors. 'We explain that though they will miss some school, that they're learning things that will help them in future life,' says Fitzpatrick. 'They learn to live by themselves, to solve problems, to travel, to cook, to organise themselves and be self-reliant. The attributes they learn from campaigning are very transferable to work.'

To address some of the education issues, the Institute of Sport is said to be at 'an advanced consultation stage' with third level institutions to introduce an Institute Performance Athlete Scholarship Scheme, which will for the first time offer elite athletes subsistence grants and funding to cover the costs of 'slow-track' study, so they can do their degree over six or eight years.

'We want to encourage our athletes to be full-time athletes, and part-time students,' says Phil Moore. 'To facilitate them studying while they're training, we need more flexibility in the third level system. We've met the presidents of the colleges and institutes and they've expressed a strong positive commitment to making this happen.' To complete the package, he says, the government must now tackle the issue of repeat fees.

Moore says it is important to think about the athlete, not as a machine for winning medals, but as a complex personality with ambitions and worries, relationships and a career path. 'They will typically retire by the time they are in their late twenties or early thirties, so they will have at least two careers in their lives. We want them to have peace of mind about that, so they can go to Olympic Games or World Championships without worrying about what will happen to them after they leave sport.' There is evidence, he says, that being involved in part-time work or study actually improves the quality of training for top athletes. It is a theory that gets a lot of support – from administrators, coaches and athletes. 'It's not always sensible or desirable,' says IIS boss Seán Kelly, 'that athletes are full-time all year round.'

The Olympic Council agrees, saying the system ideally should do more to help athletes to balance work and training. 'A lot of people leave sport because they want to be more successful in business. The trick is to keep them in sport for longer, so they can maximise their potential while being able to develop the rest of their lives along the way, progressing their career,' says

Stephen Martin, the OCI chief executive. He himself juggled sport and career, graduating from the University of Ulster, Jordanstown, in 1985 with a BA in Sport and Leisure Studies – in between winning a bronze medal with the GB Hockey team at the Los Angeles Olympics in 1984, and gold in Seoul in 1988. After college, the British hockey federation gave him a job as a development officer, keeping him in the sport, and giving him time to train.

The OCI chief says it is 'crazy' that international teams sometimes have to travel without key personnel because of their work commitments. 'What we need to do is to buy out chunks of people's time, to prepare for and compete in the key events.' The rest of the year, he suggests, players can juggle work commitments with maintaining physical, tactical and skill levels. 'This approach can often give other athletes an opportunity to compete at lower priority events.'

At the Australian Institute of Sport headquarters in Canberra, every residential athlete must either be studying or working at something. Dr Ric Charlesworth, the author of *Staying at the Top*, has been a mentor coach to several Australian national teams and has firm views about how to get the best out of athletes. 'We expected our athletes, those who were aspiring to compete at the Olympics and indeed win at the Olympics, we expected a big commitment from them. But we also understood that they had another life, and that there had to be a holistic approach about how they went about things – they had relationships, some were studying, some had jobs, they had families, some were getting married, they had all sorts of things happening in their lives. Some of them relocated, took themselves across the country to be in the programme, made considerable sacrifices to be there.'

He is himself a product of that holistic thinking. Widely regarded as the finest hockey player of the late 1970s, Charlesworth was selected for five Olympics, winning a silver medal and a World Hockey Cup. But the Renaissance man also found time to play first-class cricket, graduate as a medical doctor, and represent the Australian Labour Party in parliament for ten years. And that was before he took up coaching.

As the hugely successful coach to the Australian women's hockey team through the 1990s, Charlesworth insisted on treating his players as adults and refused to nominate captains and vice-captains – 'an anachronistic concept from a hundred years ago, in my opinion, when life was very paternalistic and hierarchical'. He adds: 'The fact that we said we were not going to have a captain on the team didn't mean that our team was leaderless – it meant that it was full of leaders and that they were all contributing.' The coach also introduced a new honour system – 'wild cards'. Any player who could not come to training, for whatever reason, could simply ring up and say they were playing a 'wild card' – no excuses were needed, no guilt was attached. 'It was about them owning the caper, really,' says Charlesworth. 'There is no point in athletes being coerced to come

David Gillick –
'We are basically
one-man companies.'
(*Sportsfile/Brendan Moran*)

to training. If they have to be coerced to come to training, better not to be there. It was just about giving them the freedom to say "Look, I need a break, I understand my body, I know where I am at" . . . you don't have to make an excuse, tell a story, anything like that, you just don't have to come that day.'

And did it work? 'What we found, of course, is that when you give them that choice, they chose to come, they chose to work hard, they chose to train diligently.' In fact, in 180 days of training with 30 athletes, just 4 wild cards were called in.

During his time as coach, the Hockeyroos won two Olympics, two World Cups and once at the Commonwealth Games, but Charlesworth says they also learned life lessons which will stand to them. 'My view was always that being in our programme was like going to university, the university of hockey if you like, but they had to learn other things too. And so we tried as much as possible to expand their experiences. Young athletes competing all around the world, going to lots of different countries representing their nation, get a wide variety of experiences and those are experiences that aren't available to everybody, so there is a bunch of pluses too, that not only do they look good on your CV, but they expand your experience and make you more employable, more interesting, widen the variety of things that make up someone.'

It is fair to say, of course, that many high-achieving Irish athletes do well out of their fame – some open pubs, or become corporate spokesmen for their industries. Others go into politics, public speaking, management training or the media. 'In sport, you have a shelf life. But you can work until you're sixty-five,' says David Gillick, who firmly believes that the sporting life is great preparation for a second career. 'What we are doing now as athletes speaks volumes about our personalities and the type of people we are: determined, focused, disciplined. We manage and source finance. We are basically one-man companies.'

Fionnula Britton agrees. The World Championship finalist is doing postgraduate research into the effects of exercise on the immune system of people with cystic fibrosis. 'Sport definitely has not damaged my education,' she insists. 'I think I find it hard to be a full-time athlete – I have to be doing other things as well. Studying probably helps me. I think they go well together. If I thought it wasn't working, I wouldn't have come back for another year to do my Masters.' Britton, who graduated from DCU with a degree in sports science, says a huge number of people in her academic field are involved in sport, as athletes, coaches or medical professionals. The two, she says, complement each other. 'You get so much knowledge just by training, it builds up over time and you do not realise it. And what I am learning in DCU, I can apply to sport.'

She recommends the dual life: 'It helps if you go to college because you have your degree. I think people who do not go to college worry more, because they do not have something to fall back on.'

No Pain, No Gain

'You would fain be victor at the Olympic Games, you say. Yes, but weigh the conditions, weigh the consequences; then and then only, lay to your hand – if it be for your profit. You must live by rule, submit to diet, abstain from dainty meats, exercise your body perforce at stated hours, in heat or in cold; drink no cold water, nor, it may be, wine. In a word, you must surrender yourself wholly to your trainer, as though to a physician. Then in the hour of contest, you will have to delve the ground, it may chance dislocate an arm, sprain an ankle, gulp down abundance of yellow sand, be scourge with the whip – and with all this sometimes lose the victory.'

– Epictetus, Greek Stoic philosopher

After a difficult training session, Sonia O'Sullivan relaxes in a bath – a cold bath, filled with freezing water and ice cubes. She stays there for a minimum of ten minutes. And, when she runs twice in a day, she bathes twice a day.

She does this to help flush the lactic acid out of her aching muscles. She does not like the experience, but she feels it is essential. In fact, to force herself to take the ice bath, she will not allow herself to eat dinner until the bath has been endured. She passes the time by text messaging. Ice

Opposite page:
Eoin Rheinisch, lucky to escape with his life after an accident in the Austrian Alps.
(*Colleen Tower*)

baths are also used by the Leinster rugby team, by world record holder Paula Radcliffe, and by members of the Irish athletics and boxing squads.

The theory is that the ice bath shocks the body's system and sends blood rushing to the core, to protect the vital organs. The blood vessels tighten, and blood drains out of the legs and arms, accompanied by waste products such as lactic acid. When an athlete gets out of the bath, the limbs fill up again with blood, invigorating the muscles with oxygen and helping the cells to repair themselves.

'The feeling? It's like daggers, being stabbed into your legs,' says David Gillick, as he settles into the icy waters beside British sprinter Martyn Rooney – two six-footers sharing a standard bath in a cold room beside the changing facilities at Loughborough University. 'It's cold, but it's the stinging for the first thirty seconds that is the most painful. It feels like your toes are going to drop off.'

Painful. But pain and discomfort are very much part of the package for an Olympic athlete. Bodies are pushed to their limits. Injuries are common. Hunger is a constant for many athletes, particularly those trying to make weight restrictions. And there are physical dangers – especially for those who must train or race on the roads.

That fact was brought tragically home to Irish sport in 2006, when triathlete Caroline Kearney was killed in France, hit by a car while on a training ride. Kearney, from Donabate in Dublin, was twenty-four, and Ireland's national champion three times (2000, 2001 and 2002). She had been training full-time in the hope of being the first female Irish triathlete to compete in the Olympic Games.

'You are not respected at all on the bike,' says road racer Nicholas Roche. 'I have been knocked down twice. The first time was at a junction – the driver in front of me realised he'd missed the turn, he swung in front of me, hit the front wheel and I went over the bonnet. I was lucky enough – there was oil on the road and I just slid across the junction on the oil, and all I did was a bit of tearing.'

Roche admits, too, that he is often frightened on long, fast mountain descents. 'Yes, I'm not the best descender in the peleton. I think too much.'

Jamie Costin, the international race walker, missed the Athens Olympics after being involved in a near-fatal car crash in Greece just nine days before his event.

'We were training in a small town outside Athens,' he recalls. 'We had just finished for the day. I had dropped off my coach and physio and I was driving up a small country road. I was hit by a water truck, broke my back in two places.'

Rushed to hospital, Costin's first thought was to ask if he would be fit for Olympic competition. He was seen by the OCI's chief medic, Dr Sean Gaine, who had him flown home immediately.

Costin never considered the possibility that he might not return to top-level sport. 'From the time the accident happened, I knew – I knew that once I had the body cast removed I would start getting back to normal. I treated it like an injury, and decided I was going to get over it.' Nearly four

Olive Loughnane went back to training ten days after having her first child. (*Sportsfile/Brendan Moran*)

months later, his bones healed and he began the slow process of rehabilitation under Limerick phys-iotherapist Johnston McEvoy. The Irish Sports Council funded his rehabilitation and continued paying his grant, even though he could not compete. 'They were fantastic in that regard,' he says.

Nevertheless, it was two years before he could compete again, making slow progress to the full walking distance of 50 km, the longest endurance event on the athletics programme and one of the most gruelling. Imagine running a marathon, then being told on the finish line that you have another five miles to go. 'It's a serious physical challenge,' says the Waterford man. 'It takes three to four months of specific preparation to race 50K.' At the 2007 World Athletics Championships fifty-four athletes started the race, but only thirty-one finished, and just twelve managed to beat the four-hour mark. 'There is fatigue building up in your body the whole way through the race. People say it's a race of two equal halves – the first 35K and the last 15K,' says Costin, who averages 90–100 miles a week in training and wears through a pair of shoes each month.

Incredibly, Costin has now fought his way back with no lasting ill-effects, qualifying for the 2007 World Championships and the 2008 Olympics. By the end of 2007, he was ranked inside the Top 30 in the world.

The physical dangers, too, are not confined to traffic. Athens Olympian Eoin Rheinisch was also lucky to escape with his life after an accident while canoeing in the Austrian Alps in 2001. Navigating a flooded lake rim, he felt his shoulder snap under the pressure of the white water. His arm useless, he could not paddle and was forced to abandon the boat. 'I got swept away, couldn't reach the bank. And I couldn't swim with the dislocated shoulder. I almost drowned.' In the swirling, glacial waters, he knew he would not survive more than a few minutes. Somehow, he made it to safety. He was rushed to hospital and underwent surgery, but it was a full seven months before he could canoe again.

Injuries, of course, are an occupational hazard in the fighting sports. Boxer Roy Sheahan, the reigning EU and Irish welterweight champion, was a hot favourite to qualify for the Olympics until he broke his left hand sparring at a training camp. He lost his fight against time to be fit for the final Olympic qualifiers in the spring of 2008. His teammate, Darren Sutherland, meanwhile, can count himself extremely lucky to still be in the sport, after sustaining a serious eye injury in May

Left to right:
Gavin Noble – 'conscious of the dangers of speed cycling on public roads' (*Gordon Thompson*); The Olympic Council of Ireland has produced a series of booklets for the Beijing Irish Olympic squad.

2006. It was a 'freak injury', recalls the Irish middleweight, which occurred in an international match against Russia. 'He threw a normal right hand . . . the right thumb of the glove caught me in the right eye, fractured my lower eye socket, my eye wouldn't move.' Now, after a successful operation to repair the damage, Sutherland has plates to reinforce the eye socket, and still suffers occasionally from double vision. Against all the odds, he has qualifed for Beijing, and has ambitions for a career in professional boxing.

Many other sports, even the non-contact events, are more aggressive than they appear to the casual onlooker. Take triathlon, for example, which begins with a free-for-all 1,500 m swim. 'You have fifty, sixty, maybe eighty guys all heading for the same buoy, a couple of hundred metres away. It certainly gets very physical,' admits Irish champion Gavin Noble. 'It's not as if you have a lane each. You are diving in on top of each other. You get pulled back by the shoulders, by the suit. You are pulling people back yourself. It's like you are on a sinking ship.'

He has been bruised and battered by the experience but says it is all part of the excitement of triathlon. 'You have to suck it up,' he laughs.

In common with Nicholas Roche, Noble has also to spend long periods on the bike – in training for the 40 km cycle part of his event. The Enniskillen man, the first Irishman to win an international triathlon – in Turkey in 2006 – is very conscious of the dangers of speed cycling on public roads. At his training base in Stirling in Scotland, he has put a 'turbo' machine into his living room, so he can train without leaving the house. 'You put your back wheel of the racing bike up on the roller,' he explains. 'We might do up to two and a half hours, me and my training partner – in front of the TV, or with the hi-fi on.'

Noble learned the value of hard work very early in life, he says. 'My earliest sporting memory is sitting in a motorboat . . . watching my dad coach a rowing team. I remember asking why one of them wasn't trying . . . he was called the cox, I was told. So any time I thought someone wasn't trying hard enough or were letting others do something for them I called him a cox . . . Mum says I embarrassed my parents a lot as an eight-year-old.'

As the modern era evolves, the job gets harder and harder. 'Unfortunately, at no stage has less training made you go faster,' says Steve Redgrave. 'In real terms, you've got to be improving, year in, year out. It's scary in some respects – where does it end?' Winning Olympic gold with Matthew Pinsent in Atlanta in 1996, the pair had to go seven seconds faster than they did winning gold in Barcelona, just four years before. In Atlanta, their 1992 medal-winning time would not have got them to the final.

In all, there are perhaps 300 Irish athletes at any one time preparing for Olympic or Paralympic competition – though many of them will not be seen until 2012 or even 2016. Of those, just over a hundred individuals, plus a couple of international teams, would currently be rated senior

Jessica Kuerten runs a stable of twenty-six horses. 'You have to keep the show on the road.' (*Sportsfile/Paul Mohan*)

is just horrendous in Dublin,' says head coach Keith Bewley. 'It means starting very early in the morning, maybe even going in at five a.m. and coming out at seven, to beat the traffic.'

'To be honest, the life is not as exciting as it might sound,' says Olympic sailing squad member Ciara Peelo, who qualified for the Games at the Women's Laser Radial World Championships in New Zealand in March 2008. 'Normally, a day consists of getting up and going to the gym and doing some training, coming back from that and just refuelling and maybe relaxing for a short while before heading out on the water for quite a long session.' The most frustrating parts of her life, she says, include the constant travelling, 'no permanent fixed base', and the endless downtime, waiting for the body to recover. 'I found that quite tough, especially in the early days. You just feel you are sitting around, doing nothing.' Injuries, too, are a huge worry. 'I missed the World Championships in 2005 with a shoulder injury. That was a kick in the teeth.'

The Malahide 29-year-old finished twenty-ninth overall at the World Championships, doing just enough to snatch the final Beijing qualifying slot. Lying a lowly sixty-fifth after Day One, Peelo fought back to make the Gold Fleet and finished strongly, ending with placings of twenty-third and thirteenth in the final races. 'Relief,' she says, was her reaction to qualifying for her first Olympics.

Keeping a world-class campaign on the road can also be expensive, especially in the equestrian and water events. Jessica Kuerten, who has been as high as No. 2 in the world rankings, has a stable of twenty-six horses 'under saddle' at her base in Hünxe, Germany. Kuerten rotates her top horses, entering each in up to twelve shows a year. But she herself is on the road all year round and must transport her mounts by road and air to competitions across Germany, Britain, France, Switzerland, Sweden, Spain, Holland and Qatar. There is 'a lot of pressure', she admits, in keeping a stable going, as she told an RTÉ documentary crew in March 2008: 'You have to keep the show on the road, so you have to earn money. You have to earn money in the ring, you have to sell horses, you have to try to find sponsors. The prize money has improved, thank God, in the last couple of years.'

Yachts, meanwhile, depending on class, can cost up to €65,000; a world-class rowing boat €22,000. Then there's the cost of transporting them around the world, and keeping them ship-shape. 'An Olympic campaign in the Star costs about one hundred and fifty thousand euro a year to run . . . coaching is a large cost, accommodation, travel, and you need a new suit of sails for every regatta,' says Maurice 'Prof' O'Connell.

Boat transport is a problem, too, for Eoin Rheinisch, who has lost no fewer than five racing canoes in the past twelve months – all of them damaged in air transit. 'I remember arriving at the European Championships last year in Slovakia. I went to collect my race boat from baggage and found it destroyed. It looked like a truck had run over it. I had to get a flight back to Ireland, get an older boat, work through the night to fix it up, and get a flight back to race.'

Agtec, his sponsors, now keep a boat at their factory, and have undertaken to crate and ship it anywhere in the world, if there is an emergency. Taking no chances, he delivered a boat to Beijing months before the Games.

Derek Burnett, a veteran of the Sydney and Athens Games, has his own particular problem with airlines as he travels the world, training and competing, en route to his third Olympics. In a world where you cannot bring deodorant on a plane, spare a thought for the man who must carry a gun and ammunition. 'I declare it, of course. But the likes of Ryanair will not take a gun, not even in the hold,' says the Longford clay pigeon shooter, who has six guns, but likes to use the same one every time for competition. Airlines who will carry the gun charge a handling fee. 'The flight might cost you eighty euro, and the gun thirty euro each way.' Even then, airlines will usually restrict Burnett to 5 kg of ammunition, or 125 cartridges – which is a problem, as shooters need roughly double that amount for a competition. So Burnett usually has to travel with a companion, who brings the other 125 cartridges. He is philosophical about the situation, but fears it is going to get worse. 'The biggest problem I hear about China is that they are not going to allow us to bring our own ammunition. That's like telling Roger Federer that he can only have the plastic racquet from the local shop.'

For track and field athletes, meanwhile, on the international circuit, there may be several months living out of a suitcase. And that brings its own issues. David Gillick explains: 'If it's a major championship, I travel with the Irish team. But most of the time, I travel on my own. Once you arrive, the event organisers usually put two athletes in each hotel room. Often I'm rooming with someone I've never met in my life. They might not even speak English. I don't mind sharing with people – usually, as athletes, we're in the same frame of mind, they're not going to be going out on a bender every night, coming home at three a.m. But sometimes it can be difficult, for instance if they put you with someone who's in the same event.

'I remember one event in Salamanca in Spain. I got to my hotel, went up to my room, and found an Australian bloke in there. Great, I thought, speaks English. We got on fine. But after a while, he mentioned that he couldn't find his camera. I helped him search the room. But I knew he was thinking I'd robbed it on him. And we didn't know each other enough to talk it out, just two strangers thrown together, both suspicious of the other. It was a tense half hour, but then he found the camera. It turned out that he'd been travelling for a couple of months, and couldn't find anything in all his luggage.'

Competing in Rome, Gillick found himself rooming with an English athlete, who had brought a Nintendo Wii to pass the time. 'He was up playing his Wii non-stop, arms and limbs going in every direction. Eventually, I ended up playing too – bowling on the Wii till ten o'clock the night before I raced.'

The problem with rooming with someone, says walking Olympian Olive Loughnane, is that people have different body clocks, and different ways of killing time before their events. She remembers sharing a room with a Portuguese girl before a Grand Prix race, listening to her chatter endlessly on the phone to her boyfriend. 'I had to put a stop to it. She had no English . . . but she understood.'

Loughnane, however, is used to distractions – she has to be, as the mother of a toddler.

Eimear was born in 2006, by Caesarian section. But that did not slow her mother down.

'I swam the day before I had her, and again on the ninth day after she was born. I did some running and cross-training on the tenth day, and went back to race walking five weeks later. I rest when she rests.'

Being a mum, says the Cork-based walker, does not stop her being competitive – certainly not with a third Olympic competition in her sights. 'I wanted to get back, I always intended to get back. But it's good to be able to walk away and have a little girl who does not know one race from another.' A typical day, she says, starts at 7 a.m. with an hour and a half's cardio walking before her husband, Martin, goes to work. She might do 17 or 18 km, or four sets of fast 3 km. She warms down on a treadmill in the house. 'Eimear gets up at nine a.m. She sits in her high chair, eating and chatting away to a sweaty mum.' After Martin comes home there is another workout – forty minutes of gym circuits, some strength training, or maybe a session on the track in Cork city.

By far the greatest distraction of all, however, according to those who have been there . . . is the Olympic Village. Often described as the greatest 18–30 singles club in the world, restricted to 10,000 of the world's most beautiful bodies, there are temptations to sway even the most single-minded individuals.

'The Village is the best thing about the Olympics,' laughs Athens sailing Olympian Rory Fitzpatrick. 'Everything is free, for a start. You walk up to a Coke machine, push a button, and a drink comes out. You see people you've seen on TV walking around the place. There is the best gym in the world. You can sit by the running track or the swimming pool and watch the fastest athletes in the world train.

'The restaurant has to cater for every cuisine in the world, from McDonald's to speciality Greek food – for twenty-four hours a day. I arrived at two a.m., starving, and I had a steak. It's a funny thing – before the events get started, the McDonald's staff have nothing to do. But, as the athletes finish, the McDonald's queues get longer and longer. They indulge in what they have restrained themselves from for four years.'

Those opportunities, say administrators, bring their own problems, particularly for athletes who are fearful and uneasy in the days before their events. 'There's a huge amount of downtime. The athletes must decide what is appropriate and what is inappropriate recreation,' says Giles Warrington, the Science Adviser to the Olympic Council of Ireland. Boredom is an issue, confirms Stephen Martin, the OCI chief executive and a veteran of three Olympic campaigns – Los Angeles, Barcelona and Seoul, where he won a gold medal with the GB Hockey team. His teammate, Steve Batchelor, he recalls, put on half a stone in three or four days in the Olympic Village, just hanging out, grazing on the free food. 'After that, our weight was monitored every day.' Learning from the experience, British Hockey introduced a more sophisticated medical monitoring system. Battling with weight, however, remains a problem for many athletes. Years later, as Team GB's Deputy Chef de Mission in Sydney, Stephen Martin remembers seeing a judo player miss her weight. 'So after a lifetime of preparation she never even got to compete!'

Derval O'Rourke – 'If a child can't handle doing sport four days a week and doing the Leaving Cert, what are they going to do in real life?' (*Sportsfile/Brendan Moran*)

Noise levels are also a problem, says Martin, and the party atmosphere builds as the Games go on, as more and more athletes complete their events and start to let off four years of steam. It's worse, he says, for those whose events come late in the games, or teams building towards finals. One British Athletics benefactor, he recalls, who was married to a Hollywood film star, threw parties every night for people who had finished.

'The Village can break your focus. There is so much going on. There is a great buzz,' says walker Rob Heffernan, a two-time Olympian. 'You really have to know what you are there for. You can waste energy.' Looking back on his first time at the Games, in Sydney, he says he has learned a lot and now knows not to go into the Village until the last possible moment. 'I was so raw, seeing everybody around you, you are starstruck. And I stayed in a portakabin. It was sweltering.'

'In Sydney I was awe-struck, going around with my mouth open, seeing people like Maurice Greene and the Williams sisters,' says another double Olympian, Derek Burnett.

By the time Athens came round, he says, he was used to it.

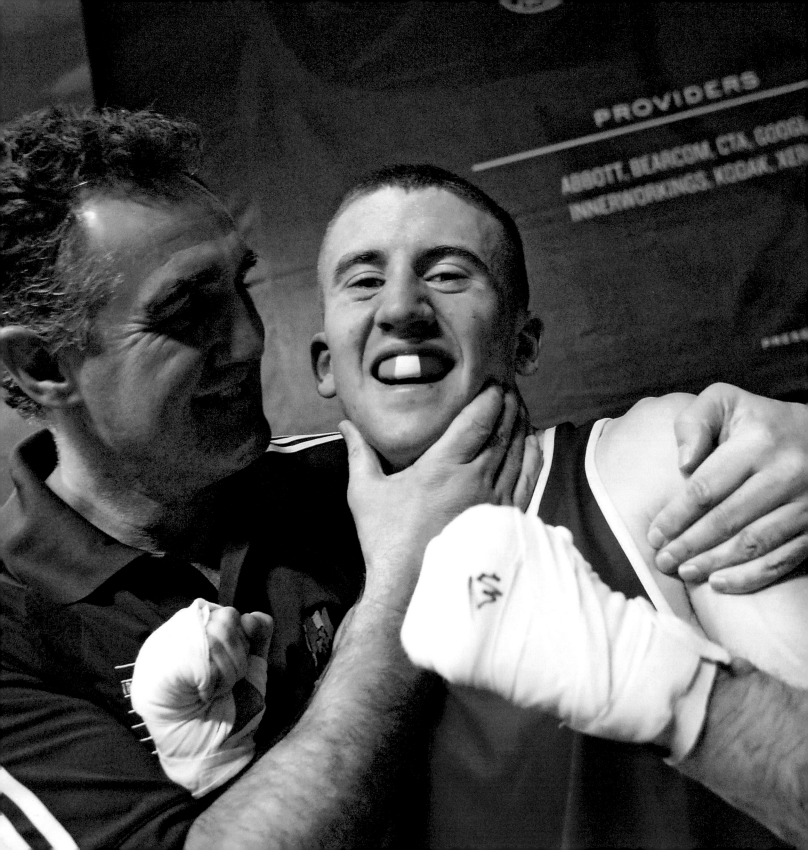

Mind Games

'I have missed more than nine thousand shots in my career. I have lost almost three hundred games. On twenty-six occasions I have been entrusted to take the game winning shot . . . and missed. And I have failed over and over and over again in my life. And that is why I succeed.'

– *Michael Jordan, basketball star*

Sport has always been as much a battle of minds as bodies. Competition is tough, athletes are supremely fit, and the margin for victory is slim. Modern managers, coaches and players realise that to get ahead they need an added resource, and that resource is a trained mind.

'When you get to an Olympic final, everyone involved in that final will have done a similar volume of training, a similar amount of build-up,' says Steve Redgrave, five times an Olympic champion. 'So what makes the difference between one person winning and one person losing? It comes down to a mental edge.'

Although sport psychology is usually thought to be a post-war phenomenon, its modern origins can be traced back to before the turn of the twentieth century. In the late 1890s, some early research was done by Norman Triplett, a psychologist from Indiana University, the first to confirm that

The Rewards

'I'm tired of hearing about money, money, money, money, money. I just want to play the game, drink Pepsi, wear Reebok.'

– Shaquille O'Neal, American basketball player

Tarry a while, and listen to a tale of two Olympic medallists . . .

The first is an American, Evander Holyfield, winner of the light heavyweight boxing bronze medal at the 1984 Los Angeles Games.

The second is an Irishman, Michael Carruth, welterweight gold medallist at the 1992 Olympics.

One gold, one bronze, one sport: but two very different outcomes.

The year after winning the bronze, Holyfield turned pro and won his first world title the year after that, adding multiple titles in both the cruiserweight and heavyweight divisions. His lifetime ring earnings are estimated to surpass $100 million.

'The Olympics is a springboard,' Holyfield told RTÉ at the 2007 World Boxing Championships. 'It's a springboard that allowed me to become the only man to be the heavyweight champion of the world four times. I had thirteen years as an amateur. I started when I was eight years old. The

Opposite page:
Sligo 5,000 m runner
Mary Cullen (557).
(*Sportsfile/Brendan Moran*)

Olympics gave me exposure. When they are looking for people to branch off to be professionals, they are looking for Olympians, someone who already has a story, a proven record that they can fight and withstand the rigours of a pro career.'

As Olympic champion – Ireland's first for thirty-six years – Michael Carruth had that proven record. He turned professional in 1994, taking leave from his job as a soldier in the Irish army. He had, however, limited success in the pro game, the highlight being the capture of the WAA world welterweight title in front of a home crowd at the National Basketball Arena in Dublin. He retired in 2000 with a career professional record of eighteen wins from twenty-one fights.

'I made money, but I didn't make millions,' he says now, without the slightest trace of bitterness. 'I have a lovely house, lovely car, but I've worked my ass off. I have to work. I have a full-time job. I still have to earn money, pay a mortgage.'

He points out that in 1992 Ireland was not the rich country it is now. And he admits he made some poor decisions. 'I should have gone to America, and fought out of America instead of the UK. I would have made a lot more money.' He laughs: 'And if I'd won track and field, I would have been a multi-millionaire.'

Now working with Des Kelly Interiors, Carruth says he cannot count the number of pints he has had put in front of him, but yet he has never been offered an official role – in boxing, or in any other sport. He expected more, he admits – as a medallist at both the Olympic Games and World Championships. 'When I won the bronze medal at the 1989 Worlds I thought my life was going to change. I think I got a bursary of between three thousand and five thousand pounds, which was spent on training camps.' But it is not, he says, something that worries him. 'If you think like that, you would become very bitter.'

Boxers, of course, have to turn professional to make the big money. Other Olympians, such as showjumpers, tennis players and track stars can cash in immediately. Ireland's Jessica Kuerten, for example, scooped a €100,000 prize in winning the Monaco Grand Prix in June 2007. A second place finish at a World Cup qualifier in Stuttgart in November earned her another €32,000. Those pay cheques, however, must be seen in the context of the cost of keeping a stable of two dozen horses and transporting them around the world.

In the big leagues, however, the rewards can be extraordinary. In its annual list of the world's highest-earning celebrities, Forbes.com estimated that, in the year to June 2007, Tiger Woods banked $100 million, more in a single year than any athlete in history. The highest-earning female athlete is tennis star Maria Sharapova, who finished the year with $3.8 million in prize money. Sponsorships from Pepsi, Nike, Canon, Colgate-Palmolive and Motorola brought her earnings to $23 million.

In athletics, meanwhile, elite runners like Paula Radcliffe can chase a prize purse of $1 million, to be split between the top male and top female champions in the World Marathon Majors series. Appearance fees, performance-related bonuses and product endorsements can also swell the coffers. A top sprinter, like the 400 m World champion Jeremy Wariner, might be guaranteed up to $20,000 just to turn up for a Grand Prix event and could pocket a further $6,000 for winning his race.

The big money in athletics is in the Golden League, the six biggest events of the year, where premium event winners attract minimum prize money of $16,000. Silver and bronze medallists receive minimum winnings of $12,000 and $9,000 respectively. Even the eighth-placed finalist will get $1,000. A bonus of $50,000 is awarded to any athlete breaking a world record.

Finally, best of all, any athlete who wins his or her event at all six Golden League meetings will share in a jackpot of $1 million. The 2007 jackpot was shared by the American 400 m specialist Sanya Richards and the Russian pole vaulter Yelena Isinbayeva, who each won $500,000.

Alistair Cragg, Paul Hession, Derval O'Rourke, Róisín McGettigan and David Gillick are among the few Irish athletes to be invited to Golden League meets. 'That's where you want to be,' says Hession, a 200 m specialist who competed at three Golden League meets in 2007. 'That was one of the highlights of my year, the quality of races I was getting into – practically every race I ran in was a race that was won in nineteen seconds, or twenty flat.'

The problem, says David Gillick, is that the meets can be a closed shop. 'Getting invited to those events has a lot to do with who your agent is. A top US agent, representing one of the world's top runners, will also have a couple of lesser guys on his books. He will offer his top star to an event, but insist that they take his other guys as well. Too often, that means an opportunity lost for European runners. But Gillick is sanguine about it: 'That's just how it works. It's business.'

Rome, in the summer of 2007, was the Dubliner's first Golden League event. 'It was a real world-class meet. There was such a buzz in the Olympic stadium, the stadium where Italy beat Ireland

From left to right: Few Irish athletes get invited to Golden League meets (l–r): Alistair Cragg, Róisín McGettigan and Mary Cullen; David Gillick in the semi-final of the men's 400 m at the 2007 IAAF World Championships in Osaka, Japan (*Sportsfile/Brendan Moran*).

in the 1990 World Cup. To describe how big it is – it's like a Champions League Final. And the absolute cream of international four-hundred-metre runners were in Rome – five or six of the guys who would later be in the World Finals in Osaka.' Drawn in lane one for the final, he finished eighth. 'Overall, though, it was a great experience. There are not many Irish athletes that can get into the Golden League.'

The Golden League culminates in the IAAF World Athletics Final, where the prize money is upped to $30,000 for winners, $20,000 for second-place and $12,000 for third. Any athlete who breaks a world record can look forward to a $100,000 bonus. Ireland's only representatives at the 2007 Final in Stuttgart were Paul Hession and Róisín McGettigan. The Wicklow woman produced the performance of her life to finish second in the 3,000 m steeplechase behind World Championship bronze medallist Eunice Jepkorir of Kenya – and collected the biggest pay cheque of her career: €20,000.

'It's the biggest lump sum I've ever won, more than my earnings from running for the last four years,' she laughs, admitting that she did not really think about the rewards until after she crossed the line. 'I knew the prize money for first was $40,000, and third was $12,000, but I had no idea what you got for second.' Interestingly, she reveals that medallists do not walk away from the event with the cash, and never see all of it. Three months later, the cheque still was not in the post. 'They have to wait for the results of drugs tests on everyone. Then they take tax from it – twenty-one per cent, I think, in Germany. And fifteen per cent goes to your agent.'

From left to right:
Róisín McGettigan won €20,000, the biggest pay cheque of her career; Paul Hession – 'Practically every race I ran in was a race that was won in nineteen seconds, or twenty flat.' (*Sportsfile/Brendan Moran*)

Galway's Paul Hession, meanwhile, collected $2,000 for his last-place finish in the 200 m final. His world-class run of 20.58 seconds also confirmed his new status in world sprinting.

McGettigan, who also made the final of the 2007 World Athletics Championships, says she does not focus on money but says it is good to feel that she is earning a living. 'I want this to be my job, so I have to expect to get money from it somehow.' In the winter months after her break-through year she was based in Tallahassee in Florida, sharing a house with members of her training group, including Sligo 5,000 m runner Mary Cullen. 'It's a lovely house, but there was no furniture in it when we arrived,' she recalls. 'The local high school coach got us chairs and a table. We got beds from people in the area. We bought a TV and washing machine between seven of us. There are five of us living in the house at the moment, but a few more are coming. There's a converted attic and two bedrooms, but we're changing two other rooms into bedrooms.' It is hardly the high life.

Triathlon – top prize is $200,000 plus a new Hummer car.

Gavin Noble at TriAthlone 2007. (*Gordon Thompson*)

One of the few Irish Olympians to make a living from his sport consistently is Alistair Cragg. He is grateful, too, for the funding he gets from the government. The problem is, he says, that 'whatever you get, you use. No one should go into the sport thinking they're going to be retiring at the end of it.' Few athletes become wealthy from their sport, he says, and for those that do, money is often an evil. 'Money can give you comforts and satisfactions, but those things may not help you running.' He is conscious, however, of the less tangible rewards that sport has given him, and of the need to give something back to sport once his career is over. 'I know I could have gone down a bad road, be sitting in a bar now, feeling sorry for myself in life. People have helped me, people have given me money when I needed it. I was sleeping on couches before I went to Arkansas, borrowing money from my brother, and I could have easily turned round and said no, running's not going to get me anywhere. I just want to teach that to people.'

Triathlon, meanwhile, is an event that has caught the public's imagination, especially in America, sucking in advertising and sponsorship. There are some ten World Cup events each year, offering prize money of around $10,000. But the biggest purse last year was a cool $200,000 plus a new Hummer car for the winner of the inaugural Hy-Vee BG World Cup in Iowa. Fermanagh's Gavin Noble is not yet at that level and nor, despite its popularity, is Irish triathlon. Noble's biggest domestic purse so far has been €3,000 for winning last year's triAthlone.

Outside the big leagues, however, many Olympic sports – rowing and canoeing for example – offer little or no prize money. And even in the professional sports, it is no gravy train. Ireland's Nicholas Roche is a professional cyclist riding with a French team. 'Money-wise, it's great when you're top, when you're winning big races,' he says. 'But for young riders, you start off on a very, very basic and low wage – considering you're only going to work for ten years.'

'Most of our pro cyclists are not getting a salary at all,' confirms Irish Cycling's Frank Campbell. Riders with the two Irish teams get basic accommodation, travel, food and equipment. 'They are there for the love of the sport, and to try to be seen by the bigger teams.' Those with continental teams are mostly on a minimum wage of €25,000, and will rarely get the chance to win prize money. 'There is a hierarchy in professional cycling,' says Campbell. 'There are those who win races and those who help the winners.'

In sailing, about a half a dozen Irish earn their living as professionals. For Olympians, however, like Rory Fitzpatrick, there is little tangible reward to show for his years in the sport. In fact, he says, successful sailors often need the financial support of their families. He retired after the Athens Games. 'I wanted different things from life. I wanted to stay in one country for more than thirty days in a row. I wanted to see friends and family, earn money, have a proper job for a while.'

Aussie Rules

It is the system that the world looks to as a template for sporting success, producing global stars such as Cathy Freeman and Rob de Castella (athletics), John Eales (rugby), Michael Klim (swimming), Mark Viduka (soccer), Glenn McGrath (cricket) and Lleyton Hewitt and Todd Woodbridge (tennis). But it has its origins in failure.

The story of one of the world's most successful sporting hothouses, the Australian Institute of Sport (AIS) begins at the Montreal Olympics in 1976 – with a crushing disappointment for the proud sporting nation of Australia, which failed to win a single gold.

Though the nation's medal tally – four bronze and a silver – would represent a good Olympic result for many nations and a spectacular success for a small state like Ireland, this was a low point for Australian sport, the worst performance in forty years, an embarrassment for a country accustomed to producing sporting champions as if by right.

'We were the most unsuccessful Australian Olympic team for . . . well, a long time. It was the nadir for Australian Olympic sport,' recalls Dr Ric Charlesworth, who won a silver medal at Montreal as a key member of Australia's hockey team.

The wider world, of course, was delighted. In the UK, the *Guardian* summed up the shock to

Opposite page:
Synchronised divers.
(*Sportsfile/Brian Lawless*)

the Aussie psyche: 'Like a middle-aged athlete gone flabby, Australia stumbled into a national identity crisis, stricken by self-doubt and torn by bitter recriminations.'

Australia's response was typically feisty: the creation of a national sports institute, aimed at re-establishing the nation's sporting pre-eminence. 'There was an inquiry held after we returned,' remembers Charlesworth. 'What was the problem? What were the issues? Why weren't our performances being sustained? And I think out of that was born the Australian Institute of Sport.'

The AIS opened on Australia Day, 1981, in Canberra, offering programmes in eight sports: athletics, basketball, gymnastics, netball, soccer, swimming, tennis and weightlifting.

The institute structure was strongly influenced by the East European model and by the American collegiate sports system. Among the first intake of athletes was Wimbledon tennis champion Pat Cash and Olympic swimming gold medallist Michelle Ford.

Today, more than a quarter of a century later, and with some 6,000 athletes having passed through their care, the AIS offers scholarships to 700 athletes across 26 sports. While the majority of the residential sports programmes still operate from the 65-hectare site in Canberra, there are also training programmes in Adelaide, Perth, Brisbane, Melbourne, Sydney and the Gold Coast. There is a new training centre in Italy, too, for Australians playing sport in Europe.

In addition to high-performance coaching, the AIS provides athletes with world-leading sports science and sports medicine services, state-of-the-art sports facilities, opportunities for national and international competition, plus the chance to travel, work and study. It also offers a national network of advisers who assist athletes with educational guidance, career planning, job searching and personal development to ensure they are equipped to deal with life after sport.

And the results? Well, they speak for themselves . . . At the 1984 Olympic Games, held in Los Angeles, Australia won twenty-four medals, including four golds. In the twenty years bridging the Los Angeles Olympics in 1984 and the Athens Games in 2004, AIS athletes won well over 100 Olympic medals, a quarter of them gold, and Australia has consistently been in the top four or five nations in the medals table.

By the 2000 Sydney Olympics, more than half of the 620-strong host team were current or former AIS athletes, and they won thirty-two of Australia's fifty-eight medals. Australia, with a population of twenty million, came fourth in the medals table with sixteen golds, after the US, Russia and China – with populations of 300 million, 142 million and 1.3 billion respectively.

The success continued into the Athens Olympics, where Australia won forty-nine medals: seventeen gold, sixteen silver and sixteen bronze – more per head than practically any other nation (though the Bahamas, Estonia and Cuba also scored highly, relative to population). More than half the golds, and 70 per cent of all Australia's medals, were won by current and former AIS scholarship-holders.

Sonia O'Sullivan (2155) races Romania's Gabriela Szabo (2832) down the finishing straight in the women's 5,000 m at the Sydney Olympics in 2000 (*Sportsfile/Brendan Moran*); Olympic gold and silver medallists, Gabriela Szabo and Sonia O'Sullivan. (*Sportsfile/Brendan Moran*)

Swimming – a sport Australia excels in.

Kevin Stacey from Dublin in action during his 800 m freestyle heat at the World University Games 2007. (*Sportsfile/Brian Lawless*)

The key to success, says Ric Charlesworth, who went on to work closely with the AIS, has been the decision to provide resources for athletes to compete internationally. 'By paying attention to supporting athletes, providing the sport science, support and assistance they need, and by increasing the quality and number of our coaches – those are the pillars of what has been a pretty successful programme.'

But here is an interesting statistic: just three of Australia's forty-nine Athens medals were won in athletics, a silver and two bronze. In an interview with RTÉ's Kathryn Davis in late 2007, Ireland's Sonia O'Sullivan, now largely based in Australia, made the point that any country that follows the AIS model needs to understand that Canberra has been relatively unsuccessful at producing athletics stars. 'It's a really strange thing – the AIS for athletics is not the big thing that people think it is,' says the former World champion. 'I don't know any good athletes who live and train in Canberra. The AIS is more for team sports than track and field.'

She has a point. In Athens, Australia won an astonishing thirty-five medals from just four sports

– swimming, cycling, rowing and diving – all largely technical events, which rely heavily on the science and technology backup provided by the AIS. Take the cyclists, for example. Long before they set foot in Greece, Australia's road racers had already ridden the entire Athens course many times, in typical hot, humid, dusty summer conditions. Not literally, but virtually, in a sweat tank built specially for them by AIS experts. On arrival in Athens they were issued with gel-based 'ice jackets', developed by Australian scientists, to manage high heat loads and prolong performance. They were rewarded with a gold medal, won by Sara Carrigan, in the women's cycling road race.

A key feature of the Canberra campus is that all the facilities have been purpose built, with unique sport-specific features. The biomechanics dome houses a two-storey laboratory, where athletes are filmed and their actions measured as they run, jump or throw. There are new physiology labs, an improved 'grunt' gym for strength and conditioning, an indoor running track and, the centrepiece, a $17-million, state-of the-art, aquatic testing and training centre, complete with two pools – a 50 m Olympic standard pool and a 25 m training pool. Said to be the world's most technologically advanced aquatic centre, innovations include start blocks that measure reaction time and force, underwater movement sensors, and cameras positioned on the floor of the pool and above the super-clear water. Swimmers, in addition, are fitted with a device called the 'Traqua', which pinpoints their location and provides physiological and performance data. Magnetic markers help scientists calculate whether a slight change in a swimmer's stroke is producing a net gain or loss in speed. Analysts can measure starts, turns, finishes, stroke length, stroke frequency, speed, and efficiency: vital information in a sport where the difference between winning and losing is measured in microseconds. At the Sydney Olympics, for example, the backup team were able to identify that Kieren Perkins, who came second in the men's 1,500 m freestyle, actually swam faster than the winner Grant Hackett – but lost the race because of poorer turning technique.

Other innovations used at the AIS include GPS computers for tracking the precise movement of rowers on the water, a synthetic indoor track with force plates sunk into its surface for measuring just how hard runners pound the ground, and a high-altitude house.

No matter how high-tech the facilites, however, no sporting system can function without a steady stream of talent. But like many other developed countries, including Ireland, Australia's population is ageing, and that reduces the number of people young enough to be potential sports stars. Fearing the economic consequences, the Australian government has issued pleas for couples to have more children: 'one for mum, one for dad and one for the country'.

Professor Peter Fricker, the director of the AIS, has said that while China can select from millions of teenage athletes, Australia has a talent pool of only 280,000 young people.

The challenge, in those circumstances, is the same for all but the biggest countries: to find new

Dr Ric Charlesworth at the Irish Institute of Sport's first international conference in January 2008. (*Sportsfile/Paul Mohan*)

talent. And the Aussies look for it in the very young. At the AIS HQ in Canberra, children as young as ten or eleven, many of them girl gymnasts, live and train thousands of kilometres from their homes.

They are well looked after – the youngsters live in comfortable quarters with their peers, attend nearby schools and are cared for by professional 'house parents'. They, like all AIS athletes, also have an army of support staff at their disposal: coaches, physiotherapists, physiologists, nutritionists and psychologists. Nevertheless, adjusting to full-time training in foreign surroundings is a big challenge.

In the knowledge that few will earn their living from sport, athletes are encouraged to develop other careers. Every scholarship holder must either be studying or working in some capacity. Under-18s must attend study hall for two hours every night and accept a 10.30 p.m. curfew on weekdays. The institute's residential scholars must also agree to their rooms being searched at any time for drugs.

Ireland, a quarter of a century behind Australia in setting up an institute of sport, has a lot to learn from its pioneering foreign cousin – about what to do, and what *not* to do. Ric Charlesworth says that in many ways Australia 'made a lot of mistakes', which other countries can avoid. 'We spent a lot of money on building facilities, which I didn't think was the way to go . . . what we did was we centralised initially and I think that was a mistake. They built a huge number of facilities in Canberra and a big edifice and . . . you know, I don't think that is the answer. It's the quality of the people and the programmes, that is the answer. I just think that was unnecessary and wasteful, we could have had better programmes rather than done that. I think that was driven by the politics and bureaucrats, rather than people in sport.'

Charlesworth maintains that the best programmes in Australia are the regional programmes, designed to suit local conditions and environment. 'For instance, no one wants to go to Canberra to swim where it's freezing cold. But in Brisbane, along the coast of Australia where people do swim and there are quality pools and programmes, that's where most of our swimmers are produced. The hockey programme is based in Perth where they have a good local domestic competition and terrific weather.'

Ireland, he says, should take advantage of its small size, bringing teams together on a regular basis.

He adds: 'We made a lot of mistakes. Other countries should not make those mistakes. They'll look at what Australia has done and they will learn from that. If you look at a country like France, they've developed their programme quite rapidly in comparison, they've had terrific results in recent times.'

The China Crisis

'In sporting terms, actually, we're all at war against China.'

– Simon Clegg, chief executive of the British Olympic Association

For a country that was in the Olympic wilderness for so long, the rise of China has been one of the great sporting success stories of the modern era.

After a more than fifty-year absence, China rejoined the Olympic family at the 1984 Los Angeles Games. The world's most populous nation announced its arrival by winning fifteen gold medals, and heralding a clear warning. Outside the top ten countries in the medals table after the 1988 Olympics in Seoul, China was the fourth-highest achiever at both the Barcelona and Atlanta games. By Sydney, it had moved up to third.

At the Athens Olympics in 2004, China finished second from top with thirty-two golds, sixty-three medals in all, pipped by the USA's thirty-six golds. Russia, Australia, Japan, Germany, France, Italy, Korea, and Britain with nine gold medals, made up the rest of the top ten.

The experience of history tells us that home advantage should lift China's medal count significantly in Beijing. Home crowds and home cooking will help, as will competing in every

Opposite page:
China take guard as Ireland's Linda Caulfield prepares to take a penalty corner in the Samsung Women's Hockey World Cup Qualifier in Rome. (*Sportsfile*)

single event, and the Chinese athletes will presumably cope better with the demanding weather and environmental conditions. But most significant of all will be the dramatic increases in spending aimed at catapulting China into top place in the medals table, toppling the USA from the spot it has held since the break-up of the Soviet Union. Shooting, diving, table tennis, badminton, weight-lifting, gymnastics and rowing are among the events in which China expects to win medals.

China's national sports programme is the envy of its competitors. There is, first of all, the massive talent pool. The world's most populous country can pick its athletes from 1.3 billion people, a staggering 200 million of whom are in the key demographic of 16- to 25-year-olds. Statistically, that would indicate that China is home to more than 2 million potentially world-class athletes. Former Danish Olympian Jim Laugesen, who coaches Ireland's sole male badminton contender, Scott Evans, puts this in stark perspective. 'China has a thousand badminton talents to choose from. Ireland has just one.'

More than 2,000 Chinese Olympic contenders, it is estimated, are in full-time training for the Beijing Games, with a little under 600 expected to finally qualify. But that does not begin to explain the extent of the resources being ploughed into China's elite sporting system, which can boast some 650,000 gymnasiums and stadiums, and which is supporting an estimated 17,000 developing athletes. In rowing alone, 2,000 Chinese are said to be at, or close to, world-class level. In Beijing, the Chinese have reportedly built a fifty-room 'nitrogen house' for their endurance athletes, to mimic the benefits of living at altitude.

Professor Timothy Noakes, author of the running bible *Lore of Running*, has been studying athletes and athletic systems for more than thirty-five years. He says it is a numbers game, and other countries will struggle to compete with China. 'I understand there are about four hundred elite British athletes being supported through their programmes, trained by the British Institute of Sport. I think there are about a thousand Australian athletes being supported. There are something like twenty thousand Chinese athletes being supported. That's the problem – there's twenty times as many athletes being looked after in their programmes. Resources are essentially limitless.'

He adds: 'Ultimately gold medals and World Cups come back to money, and if you haven't spent the money you're not going to be successful. That's what the Australians have taught us, and that's what the Chinese are going to teach us at Beijing. I think that the Chinese are going to do exceptionally well at these Olympics, because they've just spent more than anyone else has got capacity to spend. They're going to show that money in equals medals out.'

China's push for global sports domination is widely held to have been jump-started after the Sydney Olympics, following failures in the multiple medal events of swimming, track and field, and watersports. 'Project 119', China's plan to develop talent in those sports, yielded its first fruit

Karen (Huang) Bing, former Chinese international, seen here with Chloe Magee (left). (*Ed Smyth*)

at the 2004 Athens Olympics, most spectacularly on the track – where 20-year-old Liu Xiang won the 110 m hurdles, the first-ever gold for a Chinese man in Olympic track and field competition.

These days, China starts them young and bloods them early. At Athens in 2004, 80 per cent of China's athletes were Olympic first-timers – with a view, presumably, to giving them critical experience ahead of the main sporting goal, the Beijing Games. Talented athletes are identified as early as six years old and sent to provincial and regional training schools. Foreign coaches are brought in to fill the gaps in sports where China lacks expertise.

Karen (Huang) Bing, the former Chinese junior international who has now declared for Ireland, paints a bleak picture of life as a child athlete in China. She started playing at nine years old and, by eleven, was showing sufficient promise to be moved out of the family home and into a residential facility.

It was difficult, she recalls. China has a one-child policy, strictly enforced in the cities. So when she left home, it was hard on her family, and hard on her, suddenly thrown into living with lots of other children. 'I go home ten days a year, that's all,' she remembers. 'I don't see my family a lot. They try to come to visit me, but I don't go home, I don't get spoiled, I don't get taken care of. You are missing a lot of things. You don't have a childhood.'

She recalls, as a child, being made to run in the snow, wearing just shorts and T-shirt. 'We turned red. It was just ridiculous. You would be put in jail if you did that in Ireland.'

If Bing, however, sounds like she is complaining, that does not tell the whole story. She retains a certain sympathy for the strict ways of her homeland which, she says, have helped make China a world power in sport. 'It is hard. But that's what makes you strong. If you want to be really serious about your sport, you have to give up lots of things.'

Little wonder, then, that other countries are watching the rise of China with a mixture of awe, amazement and fear as rumours circulate that China may have been holding back some talented athletes from other competitions through 2007 and 2008, the better to surprise the rest of the world.

'In sporting terms, actually, we're all at war against China,' Simon Clegg, the chief executive of the British Olympic Association, told BBC. 'We're seeing the emergence of a sporting superstate

Ireland's lightweight men's four (l–r): Gearoid Towey, Eugene Coakley, Richard Archibald and Paul Griffin, at the 2006 World Rowing Championships. (*Sportsfile/David Maher*)

and it's quite frightening for all the other nations in terms of their preparations and expectations for the 2008 Games.'

Double Olympian Gearoid Towey is one who has faced the Chinese 'threat' in the cauldron of competition. He says he has been amazed by the improvements made by the Chinese rowing teams in recent years, and particularly by the lightweight four who beat the Irish into bronze medal position at the 2006 World Rowing Championships in Eton. 'In 2006 they came to two World Cup regattas and made finals – we beat them by six or seven seconds. In the World Championships, six weeks later, we drew them in the heats . . . and they pissed on us. They won the semi-final and the final. In the final, we threw everything at them. We led the race for the first one thousand [metres]. We ran out of steam. It was very mature racing, for guys aged between seventeen and twenty-three. I found it hard to believe that they went so fast. On the podium, we and the French could hardly stand. The Chinese were jumping around as if they could do it again.'

Dermot Henihan, Ireland's Chef de Mission for Beijing, suggests China could top the medals table in its home Olympics: 'I think China is going to do amazing things. In some sports, the best Chinese do not even turn up for the World Championships, because they'd get stiffer competition at home. They're on a higher level in sports like badminton, table tennis and diving. They could win three or four medals in rowing. Boxing, they're moving up. They only need a handful of medals in other sports – take medals off the US, the UK, Germany, Australia – and they will be at the top.'

In sheer population terms, says Henihan, if you compare Ireland to China, 'we shouldn't win any medals'. But he is convinced, he says, that whatever events China win, they will win them fairly. 'No Chinese athlete will be taking drugs, because if one does and is subsequently caught, they will be ostracised in society.'

What is frightening, too, for many nations, is the climate and environment that teams will face at the 2008 Games. 'Beijing is probably the ultimate in terms of environmental challenges,' says Dr Giles Warrington, Sports Science Adviser to the Olympic Council of Ireland. 'It will be hot and very humid in Beijing at the time of the Games. During exercise in the heat, about 80 per cent of your body's temperature regulation is through the evaporation of sweat. High humidity affects your ability to regulate temperature through this mechanism, as the air is already saturated with moisture. You lose body fluid from sweating, but this sweat predominantly drips off the body rather than evaporating so you do not dissipate heat as effectively.'

Dr Warrington is concerned, too, about the Beijing sun. 'Because it's sometimes cloudy in Beijing, the perception is that the sun isn't strong, but it's incredibly strong.' The Chinese themselves use umbrellas to protect themselves from the sun. Sun was also a problem during the Athens Olympics, where Irish officials worked out that by the time an Irish athlete – typically fair and freckly – walked the seven and a half minutes from the dining hall to their accommodation in the village, they could already be sunburnt. For athletes, sunburn is not just painful and dangerous – it also limits the body's ability to get rid of the heat produced during exercise.

And it could have been worse. The Beijing Games were originally scheduled to start in July, at the peak of summer, when temperatures typically reach 38 °C. Due to concerns about heat and humidity in the Chinese capital, the dates were changed in 2003 to August, when average temperatures will be lower.

'The information we're getting is that the temperatures will be thirty to thirty-five degrees at that time of year. But on occasion, it can rise to forty degrees,' says Frank Campbell, the Performance Director of Irish Cycling. His main concern is for his two road riders, who will spend six to seven hours in the saddle during the 245 km road race. 'It's a very hilly course. It starts in the centre of Beijing, then heads out seventy or eighty kilometres to the Great Wall of China, where there are seven circuits of twenty-one kilometres. That's the part we are worried about.'

In preparation for the Olympics, the Chinese capital has been building stadiums, subways, roads, railways and a huge new airport. Billions have been spent in attempts to reduce pollution, including the closure of many factories, but fears remain that Beijing's filthy air, fuelled by sixteen million people and over three million registered vehicles, could dramatically affect many events, especially endurance sports like cycling or the marathon. Even spectators could be at risk, according to the World Health Organisation, which says those with a history of respiratory or cardiovascular problems should take particular care.

The Australian Olympic Committee has said they will not send their team to Beijing until just before the Games begin, to avoid possible respiratory problems.

Ireland, for its part, will for the first time have no track and field athletes at the opening ceremony. 'We are there to compete and perform. We are not there to do ceremonies,' says Patsy McGonagle, the Athletics Team Manager. The Athletics team will acclimatise in Japan, as they did very successfully before the 2007 World Championships, and then enter the Olympic Village in two groups, four days apart, ahead of the athletics events which start on 15 August. It is a schedule that meets with the approval of the athletes. Double Olympian Robert Heffernan skipped the opening ceremony in Athens, after learning some hard lessons four years previously. 'You are on your feet for hours,' he says, 'and that's hardly ideal preparation.'

The OCI will also screen all its athletes, to find out those who might be worst affected by the pollution, giving particular attention to endurance athletes, who will be exposed for longer periods, and to the 8 per cent of the Olympic squad who are asthmatic. Frank Campbell, who has made three visits to Beijing over the past two years, including taking an Irish track team to a test event, says the air quality has much improved over that time. Nevertheless, the Irish medical team is taking no chances and has recommended the implementation of nutritional strategies designed to increase antioxidant levels naturally in the six-week lead-in to the games. 'There is some evidence to suggest that a diet rich in key antioxidant nutrients, such as vitamin C, vitamin E, beta-carotines and Omega-3 acts as a first line of defence against air pollution,' says Giles Warrington.

Another concern is travel fatigue and jet lag, which are associated with a range of symptoms including weakness, fatigue, poor concentration and loss of motivation, and therefore reduced

China's Shiming Zou, ranked number one in the world, is favourite for a gold medal in the Beijing Olympics. He is seen here in action at the 2007 World Championships against Belfast's Paddy Barnes (left).
(*Sportsfile/David Maher*)

physical and mental performance. 'The effects of jet lag are more pronounced the more times zones you travel and are more prolonged after flights in an easterly direction,' says Dr Warrington. 'When you move eight hours forward, as in the case of Beijing, your body clock is entirely out of sync. It takes about seven days to adapt to the new time zone.'

Preparing effectively is not just for the athletes. There are also the coaches, team managers and other support staff to consider – who will generally be a lot older, less fit and as a result not as well equipped to cope with the challenges facing them. In Melbourne in 1956, the Irish manager had to be hospitalised on arrival with cardiac problems. In Atlanta, the Polish Chef de Mission had a heart attack at the opening ceremony and died. Most worryingly, no fewer than three members of the British Olympic team were treated for serious blood clots after arriving in Australia for the Sydney 2000 Games. One of those was former athlete Nick Dakin, who now coaches Ireland's

The Future for Sport

In the months leading up to the 1992 Barcelona Olympics, film-maker Bud Greenspan offered a million dollars to tempt champion swimmer Mark Spitz out of retirement.

The proposal was simple. To win the cash, Spitz simply had to qualify for the Games, one more time.

It had been almost twenty years since Spitz set the world alight, winning a record seven gold medals at the 1972 Olympics. He was now forty-one.

Incredibly, using modern training methods, Spitz was able to swim *faster* as a veteran than he ever did as Olympic champion. He did not make the qualifying times, not quite – but his performance shows just how quickly the world of sport moves on.

A decade and a half later, South African Oscar Pistorius is a supreme example of the impact of modern technology on sport. His 100 m time of 10.91 seconds is over a second slower than the world record time of 9.74 seconds, held by Asafa Powell. But Pistorius is a double amputee. He lost both legs below the knee when he was just eleven months old.

Running with the aid of carbon-fibre, transtibial artificial limbs, the man who calls himself 'the fastest thing on no legs' is currently delivering startling record performances for disabled athletes

Opposite page:
Mary Cullen, second from left, at the start of her heat of the women's 5,000 m in Osaka, Japan. (*Sportsfile/Brendan Moran*)

at 100 m, 200 m (21.58 seconds) and 400 m (46.34 seconds). To put it in context, those times would have won gold in the equivalent women's races at the last Olympics, Athens 2004. His best 400 m time would have won men's gold at every modern Olympic final up to 1928.

Ireland's David Gillick, a double European indoor champion at 400 m, got his first good look at Oscar Pistorius at the Golden League track meet in Rome in the summer of 2007. 'I admit to being a bit sceptical about him and I'm entitled to be, because he'll be running in my event,' he told me afterwards.

'Let me explain. The four hundred metres is an event where, in the last hundred metres, you're fighting cramp – your muscles are engulfed with lactic acid, you think your calves are going to explode. Pistorius, he had his legs amputated below the knee when he was [a few] months old, so he doesn't have any calves, and he's not going to produce any lactic acid.'

Gillick added: 'Oscar's fastest segment is the last hundred metres – the segment that, for able-bodied athletes, is always the slowest. As we're slowing down, he's going faster. The implication is that, if we were to go on to five hundred metres, he'd probably spank us all. Then there's the carbon-fibre blades. His stride length – he bounds along, like he's on springs.

'I've heard him interviewed, though, and I thought he was very impressive, made a good case for himself. And he's obviously a talented athlete. Overall, I just don't know whether the IAAF should ban him or not. Thank God the decision isn't mine.'

In January 2008, the IAAF, athletics' governing body, said Pistorius would not be allowed to race in able-bodied events – claiming his prosthetic limbs give him an unfair advantage. The ultimate decision on whether the 'Blade Runner' can compete in the 2008 Olympics now rests with the Court of Arbitration for Sport, which was due to hold a hearing in late April 2008. 'I am appealing for all disabled athletes. We deserve a chance to compete at the highest level,' said Pistorius, who won the 200 m at the 2004 Paralympic Games in Athens. He finished second in the 400 m at the South African national championships last year against able-bodied runners.

The IAAF ruling was based on studies done at the German Sport University in Cologne, which concluded that the blades, moulded into a shape inspired by a cheetah's rear leg, constituted a technical aid, giving Pistorius the ability to run at the same speed as able-bodied athletes with 25 per cent less energy expenditure.

'We need to separate emotion from the science,' said IAAF spokesman Nick Davies. 'We all wish him well. The point here is what's going to happen in ten years? What happens if it continues to evolve?'

And that is the core issue. Not just for Pistorius, but for sport, because the influence of science is found in every aspect of modern competition and there is no knowing the extent to which it

David Gillick – 'I would love to say that every athlete is clean – but that's just not true.' (*Sportsfile/Brendan Moran*)

can evolve. When we wonder why one athlete can excel where another does not, or why we throw a football with a spiral action, we are really exploring human physiology and aerodynamics. When we argue about metal versus wooden bats, or decide which running shoes to buy, we have entered the worlds of physics and engineering. Modern athletes have their diets and training schedules designed by scientists. Materials technologists are constantly working on better footwear and clothing. Even the running tracks themselves are specially designed for maximum performance.

Today's international athletes have access to nitrogen huts, to simulate altitude; heat chambers, to help acclimatise to hot weather; bodysuits for swimming; food supplements; energy drinks. They also routinely use 'borderline' substances such as caffeine tablets, which can enhance endurance and performance; and creatine, a food supplement that serves as an energy source.

Examine Ireland's rowing boats, and you will find they are fitted with 'speedcoach' technology, monitoring the crew's speed and rhythm. The track cycling team's training bikes, meanwhile, carry a mini-computer, which measures the cyclist's power output and heart rate. At a Premiership match, behind the scenes, you will see players like Paul Scholes using a Ventolin inhaler to control his asthma. After a game, Giggs and Ronaldo will peel off heart monitors, handing them to Manchester United trainers for computer analysis of fitness and energy levels. Irish hockey is using the same technology.

Irish soccer, rugby, hockey, boxing, cycling, canoeing and tennis, among others, all use video analysis as a key part of their preparation for competition. Top tennis coaches, like the Performance Director of Tennis Ireland Garry Cahill, when they pack their gear bags for work, take a video camera and laptop along with the racquets. After videoing their players, they sit down at the side of the court and, using a special computer programme, they can instantly compare their ground-strokes, serves and volleys, frame by frame, against those of pros like Nadal and Federer. Digitised imaging has revolutionised tennis coaching – proving among other things that, in the final five feet of a tennis ball's flight, it is too close and moving too fast to be seen by the receiving player. A player strikes where they *expect* the ball to be – they do not actually see it.

Even at the amateur levels of sport, technology is invading practice pitches, gyms and sports clubs. At the local gym, fun runners are wearing chest-straps and footpods, measuring their heart rates, speed and distance travelled. Nike and Apple have combined to produce a running shoe that works with an iPod Nano, measuring your performance as you train while listening to your favourite music.

The real evolution, however, in sports science threatens to transform athletes at the very root of their being. Very soon, genetic screening will enable sports scientists to identify perhaps 80 per cent of children who have any potential to be a professional athlete. Furthermore, the testing will reveal what sport the child has most potential for, whether it be rowing, basketball, swimming or whatever.

'What most people don't realise is the incredible power of the information that lies within the Human Genome Project,' Dr Lee Silver, a Princeton geneticist and molecular biologist, has said. 'It's absolutely going to happen that during the next decade we're going to identify the genes that give individuals different athletic abilities.' Later this century, geneticists expect this knowledge to be used to create superhuman athletes. Once genes related to physical characteristics and athletic performance are identified, and gene replacement techniques are perfected, Silver says parents will be able to engineer the genomes of their unborn babies while they are still single-cell embryos.

Meanwhile, gene therapy – the manipulation of the human genome to prevent or cure diseases – may offer cheats the ultimate opportunity, the chance to become genetically enhanced athletes. Instead of using drugs to enhance performance, athletes may find a way to actually improve their genes.

Gene therapy, originally developed to treat diseases such as cystic fibrosis, muscular dystrophy, Parkinson's disease and cancer is still a highly experimental procedure performed by very few research centres. Scientists at the University of Pennsylvania, however, have succeeded in creating genetically modified mice and rats with larger and stronger muscles than their peers. Theoretically, human genes could also be manipulated to build muscles and boost endurance levels. The World Anti-Doping Agency (WADA) is taking the threat seriously and, as early as 2003, added gene doping to its 'Prohibited List of Substances and Methods'. 'We know the threat of gene doping is very real,' said Richard Pound, WADA's president at the time. 'We need to start fighting this threat now, before it becomes a reality. It is easier to prevent a problem than it is to solve it.' WADA continues to carry out considerable research in the field. 'We have been working with those who are responsible for advancing gene therapy in medicine for some years, to make sure what they are doing is not abused,' says David Howman, the current WADA Director General.

Experts predict that, in the near future, rogue laboratories will begin to offer experimental gene doping to unscrupulous sportsmen and women. Athletes, for example, who use the endurance-boosting hormone erythropoietin (EPO) would, instead of injecting the drug, inject with the gene that produces EPO, allowing the body to produce more red blood cells naturally. That, in turn, increases the amount of oxygen the blood carries to an athlete's muscles and may increase the body's capacity to buffer lactic acid.

Gene doping might also enable athletes with injuries to speed healing, or to strengthen joints or tissues, which would give them a significant advantage on the playing field.

The problem for the drug testers is how to detect gene doping. When a new gene is added to the body, it becomes part of the human genome. So how can anyone tell if a gene is new or if it has always been there?

'Those who think they can cheat using gene transfer technology will be in for a rude surprise,' says David Howman, who says researchers are looking at ways in which changes to the genome can be detected through blood testing. 'It is a priority for WADA and for our partners to make sure gene doping is as detectable as any form of traditional doping.'

The greater the rewards, of course, the greater the incentive to succeed. Athletes will always look for new ways to run faster, jump higher, recover more quickly – and, promised results, some of them will not care very much at what cost that is achieved.

Under the World Anti-Doping Code, athletes are responsible for whatever is in their bodies, regardless of the source. But despite all the warnings, scientists suggest unscrupulous athletes are taking ever more health risks as they seek performance-enhancing drugs that will not be picked up in doping tests. A recent report in *New Scientist* claims athletes are favouring substances such as human growth hormones over the more easily traceable anabolic steroids, and that many drug users go undetected.

'There are so many undetectable steroids out there that you'd be a fool to be caught. I think doping is systematic, the extent of doping is horrendous. I've become very disillusioned,' admits Professor Tim Noakes, a world-renowned exercise physiologist. He adds: 'I think WADA is making a real effort, but the reality is that the amount of money that the anti-drug organisations have to spend is trivial compared to the people who are making the new drugs.'

All this, of course, feeds the growing unease that, when we watch top-level sport, we simply cannot believe what we are seeing. That unease is exacerbated by some recent high-profile cases, such as that involving the American track star Marion Jones. Jones, the winner of five medals, three of them gold, at the 2000 Sydney Olympics, pleaded guilty in 2007 to lying about her steroid use to US investigators. She was sentenced to six months in jail and stripped of her medals. All her performances since 2000 have been deleted from the record books. Worryingly, however, Jones had been tested 160 times before the truth came out.

In early 2008, the double Olympic champion Sebastian Coe warned that athletics would struggle to cope with any more scandals. Coe, chairman of the organising committee for London 2012, called for drugs cheats to be handed a minimum four-year ban.

Ireland's Derval O'Rourke backs the call for tougher action. 'I think anyone who injects EPO into their stomach – life ban, no second chances.' And she has no time for cheats, whether Irish or international. In 2006, she recalls, she was having lunch with her late agent, Andy Norman. They were joined by Marion Jones, who was friendly with Norman. 'I just sat there and would not talk to her. She cheated the sport, cheated everybody.'

Derval O'Rourke has no time for cheats – 'Anyone who injects EPO into their stomach – life ban, no second chances.' (*Sportsfile/Brendan Moran*)

She is equally scathing about Cork runner Cathal Lombard, who retired from athletics in 2008, after returning from a drugs ban to win a national cross country title. In 2004, just prior to the Athens Olympics and following a few months of dramatic improvement, Lombard, a solicitor by profession, tested positive for EPO and was given the automatic two-year ban.

'It's not like he had a tough life, like he needed the money,' says O'Rourke.

Derval O'Rourke's tough line is shared by the vast majority of Irish athletes and officials across all sports who have been embarrassed by the very public drugs scandals of Ireland's recent past.

'Michelle Smith, Cian O'Connor, Cathal Lombard – they have ruined it for the rest of us,' says David Gillick. 'Ireland is such a small place, and in sporting terms it's an even smaller place. It paints such a bad picture for all us other athletes.'

Ian O'Riordan, of *The Irish Times*, reporting Lombard's final victory, had this to say:

'The first runner-up described what he did as "disgusting"; the second runner-up refused to shake his hand, saying, "You can't trust someone like that." And this was only part of the response to Cathal Lombard's winning of the National Interclubs cross country title. Among the traditions of the race is the roar of admiration that greets champions in their moment of triumph . . . Yet Lombard's moment in Belfast on Saturday was greeted with a deathlike silence, the sombre eyes of Irish athletics supporters not quite believing what they were seeing, or simply not wanting to believe.'

'There can never be enough testing,' says David Gillick. 'I would love to say that every athlete is clean, but that's just not true. Obviously there are still people out there who are willing to cheat.'

He is painfully aware, he says, of the damage drugs cheats have done to the credibility of sport. 'I bet you when I won my European titles there were people wondering . . . "Is he on something?"'

He gets tested, he says, 'eleven or twelve times a year'. In one week last summer, he was tested four times. 'It's completely random. Three or four months might go by without a test, then you get a series of tests over a very short period.' Home recently for a quick visit, drug testers called to his parents' house three times in the same day. 'I was at a funeral. When I came home around eleven p.m., they were sitting there having cups of tea with mum and dad, waiting for a urine sample.

'Another time they arrived at my apartment in Loughborough at eight-thirty a.m. As you can imagine, I wasn't delighted to be pulled out of bed, and I'd been tested only about four days before that as well. But I play by the rules. That's what random testing means: anywhere, anytime. I want a level playing field, so I have no problems with that.'

Many athletes, clean athletes, admit that drug tests are not something they take lightly, and they worry constantly that foodstuffs, supplements, medications – or simple errors – might somehow lead to positive results. 'I don't have one hundred per cent faith in the system. I am one hundred per cent clean and I still worry that something will happen,' admits Derval O'Rourke. She points to the example of her friend, Belfast athlete Gareth Turnbull, who took two costly years to clear his name after being wrongly accused of a doping offence.

'Everyone worries,' confirms Gillick. 'You know you are clean as a whistle, but you always wonder, in the back of your mind . . . what if?'

It is a testament to their faith in the system that so many athletes refuse to believe, as they look out across the starting blocks, that their rivals alongside are routinely cheating. 'I think some people are just that good,' says Derval O'Rourke. 'I have heard Irish athletes use it as an excuse. I cannot think everyone is on drugs. I have to work harder.'

In the months before Beijing, just one Irish athlete tested positive for a banned substance. Swimmer Andrew Bree tested positive for levmethamfetamine, a stimulant, after giving a sample at the European Short Course championships in Hungary in December 2007. It is understood, however, that the substance can be found in everyday decongestants, including the US version of Vicks Inhaler. Bree's family said: 'We believe that this negative test is the result of Andrew unwittingly taking a stimulant contained within an over-the-counter decongestant. Andrew has never knowingly taken a banned substance and abhors the use of performance-enhancing drugs.' Bree, twenty-seven, is the Irish record holder in the 200 m breaststroke and won a silver medal in the European Short Course championships in 2003. In May 2008, Jessica Kuerten was given a two-month suspension by the FEI. This followed a 2007 test on her horse, Castle Forbes Maike, which showed the presence of etoricoxib, an anti-inflammatory drug classified as a medication rather than a doping substance. Kuerten, who strenuously protested her innocence, was banned from 7 June to 6 August 2008.

In the run-up to the 2008 Olympics, the IAAF, the governing body for athletics, has promised to implement an 'aggressive testing plan'. At the 2007 World Athletics Championships in Osaka, almost 1,000 athletes were tested in the largest trawling programme ever done. Just one athlete tested positive. So is that good news – or bad? Are there fewer athletes doing drugs, or are the testers losing the battle?

'Any competitions where there are no positive tests are a step in the right direction,' says WADA's David Howman. He adds, however, that most dirty athletes are caught in out-of-competition testing. 'It's only the stupid ones who will be caught in competition.'

WADA, he says, which has a 2008 budget of $25 million, is 'keeping pace with advances made in medicine', and with new threats which have not yet become public. But he confirms that abuse of steroids, which help build muscle, is still 'a major issue', and says that cheating athletes typically use a 'cocktail' of two or more substances. There are also concerns surrounding designer drugs, blood transfusions, testosterone patches and micro-dosing of EPO. 'It is not that they have any preferred modus operandi.'

It is 'pleasing', he adds, that some big names have been caught in recent times, 'but it's still dreadful that these people are trying to cheat'.

Beijing, Howman predicts, will be the 'most tested games', with the IAAF 'stepping up' the anti-drugs campaign, and the International Olympic Council (IOC) doing 'significant' out-of-competition testing.

The Irish Sports Council, the agency with responsibility for anti-doping in Ireland, says 60 per cent of tests carried out on Irish athletes are done out of competition. ISC boss John Treacy declares his confidence in WADA, and says the war against drugs is 'not lost – it's winning and gaining all the time, but it hasn't won yet. But in terms of where I've seen it come from, in 1999, when there was an ambivalence to drug testing, it's certainly come on in leaps and bounds in the last ten years.'

Some African countries, he says, do not have the funds to set up comprehensive national testing programmes. Other nations, for whom resources are not a problem, are 'dragging their heels'. 'I would certainly be in favour of a situation where countries not co-operating fully with WADA, that they wouldn't be allowed compete in the Olympic Games and World Championships. It's action like that that would turn things around.'

Developing nations, confirms WADA, are a particular problem. Firstly, athletes who do not have access to much money or education may take greater risks, experimenting with unproven or contaminated substances. Secondly, starved of resources, many developing nations have no rigorous testing system, and therefore attract international drugs cheats who know they can base themselves there without fear of being caught. To extend the range of the testers, WADA is developing regional anti-doping organisations to serve six to ten countries. Already, there are 14 such regional organisations, covering 119 nations.

'We have achieved a lot in a very short time. We're pretty pleased with the progress,' says David Howman. 'I think we have made a difference. There is a feeling that the system is succeeding better than it was, and that comes from everybody being on board. There are five hundred signatories to the code, one hundred and ninety one countries, and all sports in the world. That is a unique body in terms of its partnership.'

Athletics and cycling, he accepts, still 'have issues that they must grapple with'. WADA is working particularly closely with international cycling, piloting a scheme called 'Athlete's Passport', which measures in an ongoing way an athlete's blood, hormonal and biological parameters. 'We have been talking about it for six or seven years. If it works for one sport, we will make it available to others.'

Ultimately, WADA believes that the fight against doping will rely on a combination of strategies,

with the current blood and urine tests supplemented by biological monitoring. Cheats will know they risk detection by having drugs in their system, or masking agents, or by biological changes which reveal the effects of doping. WADA has also introduced an internet database management system, giving the world's various anti-doping bodies immediate access to lab results, therapeutic use exemption authorisations and doping violations.

The next step, says WADA, is to persuade countries to pass laws against the trafficking of performance-enhancing drugs. 'Most countries have very few laws to prevent trafficking of the banned substances – steroids, EPO, human growth hormones,' says David Howman. 'There is more money to be made out of trafficking the banned substances than there is in heroin – and that is because it is legal. It goes on with impunity, because there are no laws against it.'

Howman makes the point that there is, of course, a bigger issue here than cheating, and that is the very real danger to drug-takers. Recent research suggests that using steroids to build bulging muscles can trigger 'catastrophic' loss of brain cells. A Yale School of Medicine study, published in

2006 in the *Journal of Biological Chemistry*, found that high levels of hormones can kill nerve cells. The drugs are also known to raise levels of the male sex hormone, testosterone, and the researchers believe this might explain why some steroid users become aggressive, even suicidal – a condition known as hyperexcitability, or 'roid rage'.

EPO, meanwhile, by thickening the blood leads to an increased risk of several deadly diseases, such as heart disease, stroke, and cerebral or pulmonary embolism. It has been banned since the early 1990s.

'The elite athletes are the tip of the pyramid,' confirms Howman. 'There are many high school kids in developed countries who are taking the stuff to get like their Hollywood heroes. There are kids dying of overdoses of anabolic steroids. It's for countries to get a hold of this, not WADA, not the IOC.'

Human growth hormone (HGH), for example, though illegal in the USA and Australia, is not illegal in Ireland or the UK. Widely believed to be the cheater's new favourite, HGH stimulates bone, muscle and organ growth. Side effects of abuse include diabetes; worsening of cardiovascular diseases; muscle, joint and bone pain; hypertension and cardiac deficiency; abnormal growth of organs and accelerated osteoarthritis. In some individuals, HGH may 'significantly reduce' life expectancy.

Nobody has yet tested positive for HGH, and it is difficult to detect because it is a naturally occurring substance in the body. Many experts suggest that, to catch an offender, blood samples would have to be taken within twenty-four hours of injection.

'There is a test in place that has been scientifically validated. It will improve,' says Howman, adding that the 'athlete's passport' system will be a great help in catching future abusers. A number of athletes, furthermore, have had doping infractions for possession of the drug, including at least six Australians.

It is widely reported, too, that one of the world's major suppliers of HGH is China, which cannot look good for this summer's Olympics. WADA has raised the issue with the Chinese authorities, who claim they are taking steps to shut the plants down. The host nation is also said to be showing signs of improving its drug-testing programmes. Having seen its advances in track and field and swimming during the 1990s halted by drug scandals, China has repeatedly pledged to embrace Olympic ideals and international standards of fair play.

London's Calling

In 1992, the then Lord Mayor of Dublin, Gay Mitchell, raised a intriguing prospect . . . what if, he said, Ireland was to bid for the Olympics?

Four years later, the Dublin International Sports Council was suggesting that 2016 might be an 'emotional year' to bring the world's greatest sporting event to Dublin.

More than a decade on and with bids now closed for the 2016 Olympics, seven cities have applied to host the Games – Baku, Azerbaijan; Chicago, USA; Doha, Qatar; Madrid, Spain; Prague, Czech Republic; Rio de Janeiro, Brazil; and Tokyo, Japan.

No mention, there, of Dublin.

What we have, however, is a far better prospect – the Olympics on our doorstep in 2012. All the advantages, without any of the costs, the risks, the disruption.

'It's the closest the Games will ever come to Ireland,' says Stephen Martin, chief executive of the Olympic Council of Ireland. A former Deputy chief executive with the British Olympic Association, he played a key role in London's bid for the Games. He wants to make sure that Ireland makes the most of its opportunity. 'We really do have to maximise it – from a sporting, national, tourism and business perspective.'

Opposite page:
Melanie Nocher –
breaking records
once held by
Michelle Smith de Bruin.
(*Sportsfile/Brian Lawless*)

Statistics show that there is a huge host country advantage at the Games. Traditionally, the home country wins about three times their usual percentage of medals, and about twice their average in the Games immediately before and after their home Games.

> There is also evidence that the mix of medals is richer, with home teams winning a proportion of gold medals higher than both their historical average and the proportion available.
>
> – Clarke, S. R. (2000), 'Home Advantange in the Olympic Games'

London first held the Olympics in 1908, when Britain topped the medals table. On the second occasion, in 1948, they came twelfth. The Greek team gave their best performance in more than a century when their country hosted the 2004 Games in Athens, finishing in fifteenth place. In the soccer World Cup, host-country winners include England in 1966, West Germany in 1974, Argentina four years later and France in 1998.

For London in 2012, Britain's stated aim is to finish fourth in the medals table. To do that, Team GB will essentially have to double the number of gold medals it won in Athens in 2004, where it finished tenth in the medal table with nine golds, nine silvers and twelve bronze.

'Virtually every city that stages the Games sees a good boost for their home team in the Olympics that follows,' London mayor Ken Livingstone, who pushed for the capital to host the Games, told reporters at an Olympic media briefing in 2007.

British Olympic Association chief executive Simon Clegg, meanwhile, told BBC Sport that Britain could expect a real medal bounce from 2012. 'Spain had won four gold medals in the history of the Olympic movement from 1896 up to and including 1988. When they hosted in Barcelona in 1992, they delivered thirteen.'

For Ireland, as next-door neighbour, the challenge is to see if we can 'piggyback' on some of this ambition. For once at the Olympics, we won't have to deal with international travel, heat, language difficulties, or changes in season, time zones, food and culture. Travelling fans should also ensure supportive crowds.

'It's the same climate, the same food. No one is going to have to move away to train,' says Olympic champion Michael Carruth. In the build-up to the Games, he predicts, countries like the USA and Cuba are going to want to base themselves in Ireland.

'This is a once-in-a-lifetime real opportunity to use this as an additional catalyst to move high-performance sport on,' says Stephen Martin of the OCI. 'We have to use it as a catalyst to make a change in thinking, in our funding, in our approach to high-performance sport. There are signs of that happening, but obviously we'd like to see it happen quicker.'

The current government investment in high-performance sport (€9 million in 2008) is, he says, 'inadequate' if we are to be successful at world and Olympic level. He calls for a 'longer-term view', where there are two parallel streams of funding: one for the current Olympics, and one for the Games after that. 'There would be some crossover obviously, as some athletes will go to two Games. But you have to have that consistency of approach in personnel and consistency of performers coming through the system.' There should also, he says, be 'a strategic approach' to the development of training facilities and the targeting of international events.

Left to right:
Ailis McSweeney, from Carrigtwohill, County Cork, crosses the finish-line with a season's best time of 11.92 seconds in 100 m in Bangkok, Thailand, 2007 (*Sportsfile/Brian Lawless*); Ireland's Tara McMahon battles Kathleen Radtke of Germany for possession at the World University Games 2007. (*Sportsfile/Brian Lawless*).

He points to the British system, which last year announced an increased budget for the London 2012 Games of £600 million for the preparation of Team GB. UK Sport has estimated it costs £70,000 (€93,000) a year to fund the training programme of a medal-winning athlete, and £40,000 to train a developing athlete.

'If we're serious about it here, there are a number of essentials ingredients that need to be addressed,' says Martin. 'We need to establish a clear and shared vision for Olympic sport, and

develop a "no compromise" approach and funding to achieve it. We need to establish a systematic approach to identifying and maximising the potential of our best athletes and develop concurrent athlete programmes for 2008 and 2012. Finally, we need to recruit world-class coaches to work in Ireland, whilst developing our talented Irish coaches.'

Some sports will need small numbers of support staff, some sports larger numbers, he says, adding that the Institute of Sport should provide the 'added value', in terms of science and medical back-up, lifestyle support and talent identification. 'The most effective way of delivering a world-class system that we can be proud of is through a strong partnership between the Olympic Council and an independent Irish Institute of Sport.'

Dermot Henihan, the Chef de Mission of the Irish Olympic team, says Ireland 'should have started planning for London four years ago'. He would like to see a much greater emphasis on talent identification, not just for London but for 2016 as well. Experts, he says, already know what size and shape is needed for various sports. 'We should be identifying people, pushing them towards sports they are suited to. The athletes who will go to the Games of 2016 are already born.' He instances the British champion diver Tom Daley, who will be just fourteen when he makes his debut in Beijing, making him Britain's second youngest male Olympian.

Seán Kelly, the executive chairman of the Irish Institute of Sport predicts that, by the time of the 2012 Olympics, Ireland will be represented by a bigger Irish team and will compete in 'a few more sports' – including hockey, soccer and more relay events. 2012, he says, will also be a great opportunity to showcase Ireland. International teams will come here to acclimatise, and there will be spin-offs for tourism. 'London is probably going to be the biggest event we have ever had – as close to home as we will ever get.'

The government, for its part, set up a task force in 2006 to examine the possible opportunities that the London Olympics might offer Ireland in the areas of business, tourism and sport. A statement on the website of the Department of Arts, Sport and Tourism says officials have been doing an audit of facilities that might be developed to meet the training needs of overseas teams. 'Any expenditure on facilities will be aimed not only at attracting teams but also at ensuring a lasting legacy for Irish sports, particularly in encouraging greater participation in Olympic sports. We are also examining the possibility of attracting qualifying tournaments to Ireland.'

The OCI President, Pat Hickey, is a member of the government's task force. He has very firm views on the opportunity that 2012 presents. 'If we do not leave a legacy of sporting infrastructure after the London Games, we are finished. Ireland has practically the worst sporting infrastructure in Europe. Croatia would put us to shame. They're not long out of a brutal civil war, they have the same population, and they are light years ahead. Malta and Cyprus have better facilities than we do.'

'The opportunity is there if they put facilities in place now,' agrees Irish sprinter Joanne Cuddihy, now training in the UK. 'London is an hour from Dublin. Countries will come. But they have to build now.'

The OCI chief, who once famously remarked that Dublin could not provide the toilet facilities for the Olympics, maintains that it is 'practically impossible' for a country with a population of less than twelve million to host the Games. He points out that a bid-winning city needs massive investment and huge numbers of volunteers. 'We were never going to have it with four million people. We would not have anything like the facilities.'

Ireland, he says, has no arena capable of hosting a full international gymnastics tournament, and he is particularly critical that some major sports centres being built around the country do not meet Olympic standards. He says the planning, so far, for the London Games has been 'poor', and insists there should be more done to help young athletes make the grade.

Regardless of the legacy, however, London looks set to be a very significant opportunity for Ireland. Quite a large number of the current Olympic squad will be young enough to compete in 2012.